SCIENCE PROCESS SKILLS

Assessing Hands-on Student Performance

Dr. Karen L. Ostlund

Dale Seymour Publications®
Parsippany, New Jersey

Dale Seymour Publications
An imprint of Pearson Learning
299 Jefferson Road, P.O. Box 480
Parsippany, New Jersey 07054-0480
www.pearsonlearning.com
1-800-321-3106

Managing Editor: Michael Kane
Project Editor: Mali Apple
Production: Karen Edmonds
Design: Vicki Philp
Illustrations and Cover Art: Rachel Gage

Dale Seymour Publications® is a registered trademark of Dale Seymour Publications, Inc.

ISBN 201-29092-8

11 12 ML 02 01 00

This Book Is Printed
On Recycled Paper

CONTENTS

THE PROCESS SKILLS

Skill	Level 1	2	3	4	5	6
Observing Using one or more of the five senses to gather information. May include the use of equipment.	X	X	X	X	X	X
Communicating Giving or exchanging information verbally, orally, and/or in writing.	X	X	X	X	X	X
Estimating Approximately calculating a quantity or value based on judgment.	X	X	X	X	X	X
Measuring Comparing objects to arbitrary units that may or may not be standardized.	X	X	X	X	X	X
Collecting Data Gathering information about observations and measurements in a systematic way.	X	X	X	X	X	X
Classifying Grouping or ordering objects or events according to an established scheme. Based on observations.	X	X	X	X	X	X
Inferring Developing ideas based on observations. Requires evaluation and judgment based on past experiences.	X	X	X	X	X	X
Predicting Forming an idea of an expected result. Based on inferences.	X	X	X	X	X	X
Making Models Developing a physical or mental representation to explain an idea, object, or event.	X	X	X	X	X	X
Interpreting Data Reading tables, graphs, and diagrams: Explaining the information presented in a table, a graph, or a diagram (including maps), and/or using it to answer questions.			X	X	X	X
Making Graphs Converting numerical quantities into a diagram that shows the relationships among the quantities.			X	X	X	X
Hypothesizing Stating a problem to be solved as a question that can be tested by an experiment.			X	X	X	X
Controlling Variables Manipulating one factor that may affect the outcome of an event while other factors are held constant.			X	X	X	X
Defining Operationally Stating specific information about an object or phenomena based on experiences with it.			X	X	X	X
Investigating Using observations to collect and analyze data to draw conclusions in order to solve a problem.			X	X	X	X

INTRODUCTION

Science is more than a body of facts, a collection of principles, and a set of tools for measurement. Science is a structured and directed way of asking and answering questions. It is a pedagogical feat to teach students the facts of science and technology; it is a pedagogical triumph to teach students these facts in their relation to the procedures of scientific inquiry.

The intellectual value of mastering the science process skills is far greater than the value of the ability to repeat scientific facts or principles. The processes of scientific inquiry, learned not as a set of rigid rules but as ways of finding answers, can be applied without limit. To be effective, methods for testing student achievement must provide students with hands-on materials and the opportunity to demonstrate their use of science process skills.

The process skill assessments in this book provide an effective method for testing student achievement, and provide the teacher with feedback on pupil performance. Each appraisal is designed to give teachers information concerning each student's knowledge of a particular process skill and use of that knowledge.

It is important to keep in mind that several process skills may be used in the mastery of a particular process skill. Although one process skill is being appraised for mastery in each activity, the student is often demonstrating mastery of several process skills at once. For example, when a student uses the process skills of classifying or inferring, the process skill of observing is also incorporated.

PROCESS SKILLS AND INTELLECTUAL DEVELOPMENT

The process skills form the basis of human learning and set humans apart from other animals. Scientists use the process skills whenever they define scientific concepts or develop taxonomies. We use them whenever we speak, hear, read, write, or think as we mentally structure sensory input from our environment. In an attempt to understand our world, we have become proficient in using these process skills, making them the most powerful tools we have for producing and arranging information about our world.

In the early stages of development, children tend to be perceptually oriented and are able to sort objects on the basis of single characteristics. These early organizational abilities, such as sorting and grouping, appear to be preliminary and necessary for effective conceptualization to take place. Therefore, the basic process skills of observing, communicating, estimating, measuring, collecting data, classifying, inferring, predicting, and making models are introduced and practiced in Level 1 and Level 2.

The ability to group objects by single perceptual characteristics becomes less important in the child's organizational repertoire as the child acquires the ability to group by more than one characteristic simultaneously or to group by abstract characteristics. Although early abilities recede into the background, they never completely disappear. The basic process skills become incorporated with more advanced levels of thinking. More effective forms of organizing replace them, but an individual may return to basic process skills when grappling with a "new" situation. Therefore, we reinforce the nine basic process skills in Levels 3 through 6 and introduce and practice the integrated process skills of interpreting data, making graphs, formulating hypotheses, controlling variables, defining operationally, and investigating.

Keep in mind that students may not master process skills at a constant and continuous rate. It is reasonable to expect plateaus in which newly acquired process skills become integrated, used, and made functional. As students develop process skills, they pass through ways of thinking, each representing a different organization of experience, information, and knowledge, and each leading to a very different view of the world. As you provide your students with experiences to use process skills, challenge them to use a particular skill with different materials at various levels of abstraction without the progressive requirement of being at a more advanced developmental stage. This allows students at an identified stage of development to explore many experiences within that stage.

One student's progress should not be compared with the progress of other students. The teacher's role is to select worthwhile experiences appropriate to a student's developmental level, organize them for meaningful interpretation, and orchestrate them to provoke thought. Experiences designed to use thinking capabilities may provide significant cognitive and affective benefits by allowing students to perform progressively challenging tasks that are within their realm of potential success.

USING THE ASSESSMENTS

The assessments can be used in a variety of classroom settings. Multiple stations could be set up so that each student is encouraged to focus on his or her own work free from distractions. The arrangement of the stations will influence the quality of each student's work and the monitoring the teacher will have to do while students complete each task. One way to provide focus and reduce distractions is to set up carrels or partitions on tables or desks. Arranging tables or desks to face away from each other will also facilitate the appraisal process.

The assessments are designed to be flexible enough to be administered individually, in a small group, or with the entire class. It is recommended that not all assessments be used at one sitting because the tasks take more time to complete than standardized tests.

The assessments are designed to meet the needs of both teachers and students. The suggested levels are arbitrary labels which are dependent on the amount of practice students have had in using science process skills. Teachers may want to start with the observing task labeled Level 1 and continue through the Level 2 through 6 observing tasks to determine the students' level of development in a particular skill. Also, teachers may use the same data sheet for a particular skill, but give students a different set of objects to manipulate; e.g., instead of having students classify rocks for a particular data sheet, have them classify shells.

The value of the science process skill assessments is enhanced by the enjoyment and success students derive from completing the tasks. The assessments evaluate one of the principal objectives in science: helping students acquire competence in the use of the process skills. They demonstrate the important role of assessment in determining precisely what individual students are able to **do** as a result of their science experiences.

OBSERVING

Materials
Observing assessment sheet
crayons
6 pairs of buttons (12 in all) in a reclosable bag
(suggested set of buttons: 2 small 2-hole
red buttons, 2 small 4-hole red buttons,
2 large 2-hole red buttons, 2 large 4-hole
red buttons, 2 small 2-hole blue buttons,
2 large 4-hole blue buttons)

Procedure
Have the student observe the buttons. Tell the
student that for each button there is a matching button. Ask the student to place each pair
of matching buttons in one of the boxes on
the assessment sheet. Have the student trace
around the matching buttons, color them, and
draw dots to show the holes in each button.

COMMUNICATING

Materials
Communicating assessment sheet
crayons

Procedure
Have the student draw a picture in each box
of an animal that moves in each of the following ways: walks, swims, crawls, and flies.

ESTIMATING

Materials
Estimating assessment sheet
centimeter ruler

Procedure
Have the student look at the centimeter ruler.
Explain that a finger is about one centimeter
wide. Have the student estimate the length of
each line in centimeters using his or her
finger. Ask the student to record the estimate
in the box next to each line.

MEASURING

Materials
Measuring assessment sheet
14 paper strips cut from an assortment of
colored paper (suggested set of strips:
3 strips of different colors 4 cm × 1 cm,
2 strips of different colors 6 cm × 1 cm,
4 strips of different colors 8 cm × 1 cm,
5 strips of different colors 2 cm × 1 cm)
glue

Procedure
Ask the student to place strips of equal length
in the same box on the assessment sheet.
Then have the student glue down the strips.

COLLECTING DATA

Materials
Collecting Data assessment sheet
20 colored squares (2 cm × 2 cm) in a
reclosable plastic bag (suggested set of
squares: 4 red squares, 5 blue squares,
2 yellow squares, 3 green squares, 6 orange
squares)
glue

Procedure
Have the student sort the squares into piles
according to color. Then ask the student to
arrange all the squares of the same color in a
column on the assessment sheet. Have the
student glue the squares down. Then ask the
student to count the squares in each column
and write the number in circle below each
column.

CLASSIFYING

Materials
Classifying assessment sheet
10 small stones in a reclosable plastic bag
crayons

Procedure

Have the student sort the stones into two groups by placing the stones in the circles. Tell the student to trace around the stones and color them. Ask the student how the stones in each group are alike. Then ask how the stones in each group are different. Write down student responses. (You may want students with adequate writing skills to write their own responses.)

INFERRING

Materials

Inferring assessment sheet
sock containing a small object such as a
    peanut (do not use sharp objects)
crayons

Procedure

Have each student place one hand into the sock and feel the object. Ask the student to describe how the object feels. Record the responses on the data sheet. (You may want students with adequate writing skills to write their own responses.) Then have the student draw a picture of what the object in the sock might look like.

PREDICTING

Materials

Predicting assessment sheets
small box without a lid
5 rubber bands of equal length but
    different thicknesses
tape
crayons

Procedure

Have the student stretch the thinnest rubber band around the box, pluck it, and observe the pitch. Then have the student stretch the thickest rubber band around the box, pluck it, and observe the pitch. Have the student predict the order of the three remaining rubber bands from highest to lowest pitch, and trace around and color them in the predicted order in the first set of boxes.

Have the student test the predictions, and then tape the rubber bands on the data sheet from highest to lowest pitch produced. Have the student compare the predicted order with the actual order.

MAKING MODELS

Materials

Making Models assessment sheet
supplies such as:
    pipe cleaners
    construction paper
    scissors
    tape
    glue
crayons

Procedure

Ask the student to make a model of a plant from the supplies. Have each student attach the plant model to the assessment sheet with tape, cut the labels from the bottom of the sheet, and label parts such as the root, stem, flower, fruit, seed, and leaf.

OBSERVING

1. Put a pair of matching buttons in each box.

2. Trace around the buttons.

3. Color the buttons and draw dots to show the holes.

COMMUNICATING

Draw a picture of an animal that moves in each way.

Walks	Swims
Crawls	Flies

ESTIMATING

1. Use your finger to estimate how long each line is in centimeters.

2. Write the number in the box.

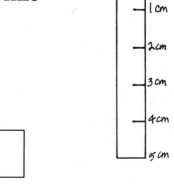

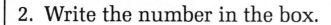

MEASURING

1. Place the strips that are the same length in the same box.

2. Glue down the strips in each box.

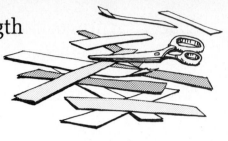

COLLECTING DATA

1. Put the squares that are the same color in the same column.

2. Glue the squares down.

3. Count the squares in each column and write the number in the circle below each column.

Name _____

CLASSIFYING

1. Sort the stones into two groups in the circles below.

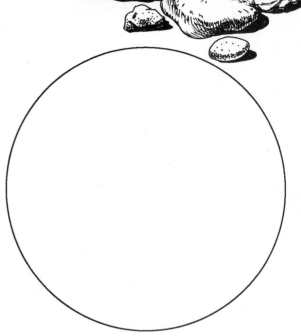

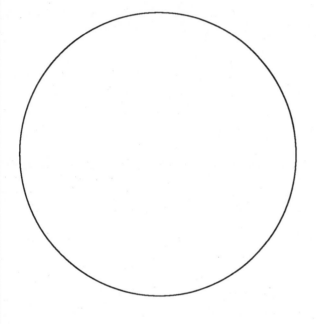

2. Trace around the stones and color them.

3. How are the stones in the two groups different?

_____

_____

_____

4. How are the stones in each group alike?

_____

_____

_____

8

Level 1

INFERRING

1. Put your hand in the sock.

2. How does the object feel?

_____

_____

_____

_____

3. Draw a picture of how you think the object
   in the sock looks.

PREDICTING

1. Stretch the thinnest rubber band around the box and pluck it.

2. Do the same thing with the thickest rubber band.

3. In the boxes, put the rubber bands in order from the highest to the lowest sound you think they would make. Trace around them and color them.

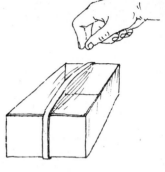

highest pitch

lowest pitch

4. Now test all the rubber bands.

5. Tape the rubber bands into the boxes in order from the highest to lowest sound they made.

highest pitch

lowest pitch

6. Are the rubber bands in the same order as your drawings?

Yes _____   No _____

MAKING MODELS

1. Make a plant model from the materials.

2. Tape your plant model below.

3. Cut out the labels.

4. Label the parts of your plant.

| root | stem | flower | fruit | seed | leaf |

OBSERVING

Materials
Observing assessment sheet
5 nuts of the same kind per student
   (suggested nuts: walnut, Brazil nut,
   acorn, pecan, peanut, almond, filbert)
crayons or markers

Procedure
Have the student select a nut from the group of five. Ask the student to observe it using the senses of sight and touch and to describe its color, shape, size, texture, and special features. Record responses. (Students with adequate writing skills can complete the assessment sheet on their own.) Mix the selected nut with the other four. Ask the student to find it and to describe the features that helped in finding it.

COMMUNICATING

Materials
Communicating assessment sheet
3 apples (1 whole apple, 1 cut horizontally,
   and 1 cut vertically)
crayons or markers
lemon juice (to keep cut apples fresh)

Procedure
Have the student observe the whole apple and draw it. Then have the student observe the vertically cut apple and draw a diagram to show what the apple looks like inside. Finally, have the student observe the horizontally cut apple and draw a diagram of this cross section. Ask the student to describe an apple from the inside to the outside. Record student responses on the data sheet. (Students with adequate writing skills can complete it on their own.)

ESTIMATING

Materials
Estimating assessment sheet

1 centimeter square piece of paper or cardboard

Procedure
Explain that the square is a centimeter long on each side and that it can be used to estimate surface area by placing it on a figure's surface and estimating how many square centimeters would cover the surface. Ask the student to use the square to estimate the number of square centimeters that would cover each figure on the assessment sheet, and to write each estimate in the circle next to the figure.

MEASURING

Materials
Measuring assessment sheet
6 containers of various sizes numbered 1–6
100-ml measuring cup
water

Procedure
Ask the student to arrange the containers from smallest to largest capacity. Then have the student use the 100-ml measuring cup as a standard unit of measure to determine the volume of each container by counting the number of cups required to fill each. Have the student record the number of cups of water used to fill each container. Ask the student to order the containers from smallest to largest based on the number of cups of water each container held. Then ask the student to compare the results to the original estimate of the order of the containers.

COLLECTING DATA

Materials
Collecting Data assessment sheets
30 buttons of the same size but different
   colors (use a different number of buttons
   for each color; e.g., 8 white, 6 black,
   4 red, 2 blue, 7 pink, 3 yellow)
   Note: Buttons should be the same size or

smaller than the squares in the graph paper.
crayons or markers (in colors corresponding
to the colors of the buttons)

Procedure
Have the student sort the buttons into piles
according to color, and then arrange all the
buttons of the same color in one column. Have
the student color the squares containing red
buttons red, etc. Then ask the student to count
the squares colored in each column and write
the number in the circle below each column.
Have the student determine from the graph for
which color he or she had the most buttons
and for which color he or she had the least.

CLASSIFYING

Materials
Classifying assessment sheets
penny
nickel
dime
quarter *(Note: Select some coins with the
same date.)*

Procedure
Ask the student to sort the coins into two
groups and place them in the two circles. Tell
the student to trace around each coin. Ask the
student how the two groups of coins are different. Record responses. (Students with adequate writing skills can complete the assessment sheet on their own.) Ask the student to
sort the coins into two groups in a different
way, trace around each coin, and explain how
the two groups of coins are different. Ask the
student how all four coins are alike (e.g., shape,
round, circles, money, coins, all have dates).

INFERRING

Materials
Inferring assessment sheet
triangles, circles, rectangles, and squares cut
from one color of construction paper
*(Note: Use assessment sheet to make
patterns for the shapes)*
crayons or markers

Procedure
Have the student place the construction paper
shapes on top of the drawings in each row.
Ask the student to observe the pattern in each
row and infer what shape would come next.
Ask the student to draw and color the next
shape in the box at the end of each row.

PREDICTING

Materials
Predicting assessment sheet
100 paper clips
4 magnets
masking tape

Procedure
Ask the student to place one magnet in a pile
of 100 paper clips, count the number of paper
clips that stick to it, and record this number.
Then have the student stick three magnets
together (using tape if necessary) and repeat
the procedure.

Ask the student to predict how many clips
two magnets will pick up and how many four
will pick up. Record the predictions. Have the
student test the predictions by picking up
paper clips with two and four magnets and
recording the actual number picked up by
each set. Ask the student what information
was used to make the predictions.

MAKING MODELS

Materials
Making Models assessment sheet
scissors
paper clip

Procedure
Have the student cut out the model of a
winged seed on the solid lines. Ask the
student to fold the paper on the dotted lines
and attach a paper clip to the bottom. Then
have the student drop the paper model and
observe its motion. Ask each student to
explain how this model shows the way the
wind carries seeds.

OBSERVING

1. Use your eyes and hands to observe one of the nuts.

2. Describe the nut.

   Color _____

   Shape _____

   Size _____

   Texture _____

   Special features _____

3. Draw a picture of your nut in the box.

4. Mix your nut with the other nuts.

5. Find your nut and draw it in the box.

6. Describe the features that helped you find your nut.

   _____

   _____

   _____

COMMUNICATING

1. Draw and color a picture of the whole apple.

2. Draw and color a picture to show the inside of an apple cut from the top to the bottom.

3. Draw and color a picture to show the inside of an apple cut across the middle.

4. Describe an apple from the inside to the outside.

_____

_____

_____

ESTIMATING

1. Use the square to estimate the number of square centimeters in each of the shapes below.

2. Write your estimate in the circle next to the shape.

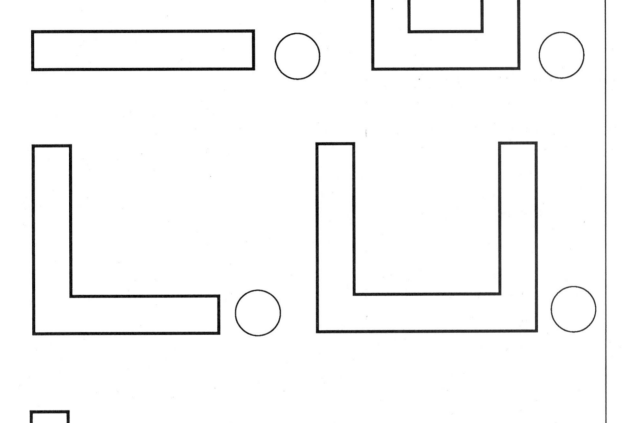

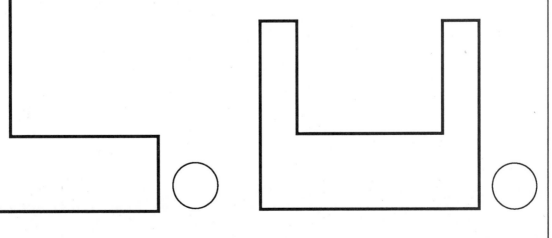

MEASURING

1. Estimate the order of the containers from smallest to largest. Write the number of each container on the lines in order.

   Smallest ─────────────────────────→ Largest

   _____   _____   _____   _____   _____   _____

2. Use the measuring cup to fill each container with water. Write the number of cups used to fill each container.

   Container 1 _____   Container 4 _____

   Container 2 _____   Container 5 _____

   Container 3 _____   Container 6 _____

3. Arrange the containers in order from smallest to largest. Write the number of each container in order.

   Smallest ─────────────────────────→ Largest

   _____   _____   _____   _____   _____   _____

4. Compare your estimate to the number of cups each container held. Which containers surprised you?

   _____

   _____

   _____

COLLECTING DATA

1. Sort the buttons into groups by color.

2. Place all the buttons of the same color in a column on the grid.

3. Color the squares covered by a button the same color as the button.

4. How many buttons are in each column? Write the number in the circle below the column.

5. Of which color was the greatest number of buttons?

_____

6. Of which color was the least number of buttons?

_____

Level 1

CLASSIFYING

1. Sort the coins into two groups in the circles below.

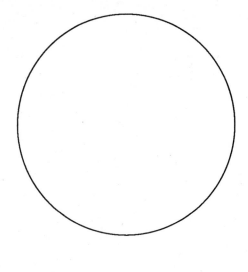 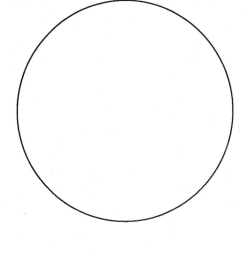

_____   _____
Label   Label

2. Trace around each coin.

3. Label each group.

4. How are the coins in each group different?

_____

_____

_____

5. Sort the coins into two groups in a different way.

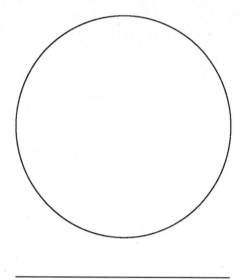 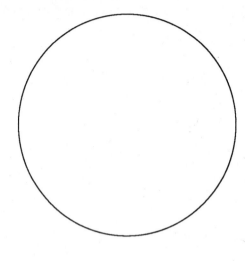

Label   Label

6. Trace around each coin.

7. Label each group.

8. How are all four coins alike?

_____

_____

_____

INFERRING

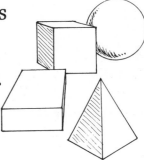

1. Place the paper shapes on top of the drawings in each row.

2. Look at the pattern of the shapes in each row.

3. In the box at the end of the row, draw the shape that comes next.

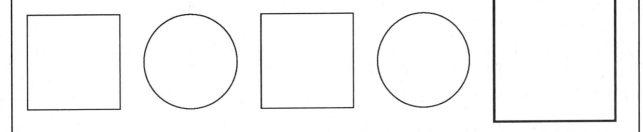

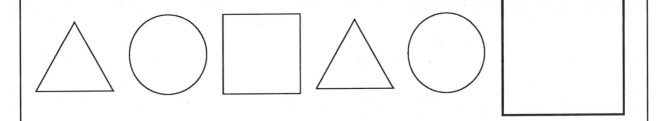

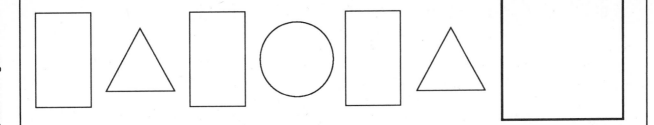

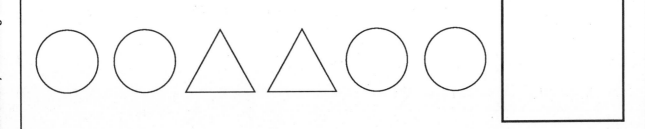

PREDICTING

1. Push one magnet into a pile of 100 paper clips.

2. Count the number of paper clips that stick to the magnet.

3. Record the number in the box.

4. Stick three magnets together (use tape if necessary) and push them into a pile of 100 paper clips.

5. Count the number of paper clips that stick to the magnets.

6. Record the number in the box.

7. Predict how many paper clips will stick to two magnets.

8. Predict how many paper clips will stick to four magnets.

9. Record the actual number of paper clips that stick to two magnets.

10. Record the actual number of paper clips that stick to four magnets.

11. What information did you use to make your predictions?

_____

_____

_____

MAKING MODELS

1. Cut out the winged seed model on the solid lines.

2. Fold it on the dotted lines.

3. Attach a paper clip to the bottom.

4. Drop the seed model and observe its movement.

5. How does your model show how wind carries seeds?

_____

_____

BOTTOM

FOLD UP

FOLD DOWN

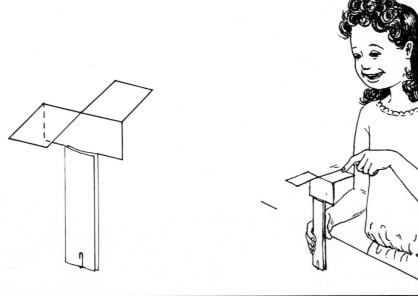

LEVEL 3

OBSERVING

Materials
Observing assessment sheet
2 bar magnets
2 paper clips

Procedure
Ask each student to touch the end of one magnet to a paper clip and observe what happens. Then have the student place the magnet on the table and touch one end of a paper clip to several places along the sides and at the ends of the magnet. Record observations. Ask the student to slide the second magnet towards the magnet on the table and observe what happens as the N (north) poles approach each other, and then as the N and S (south) poles of the two magnets approach each other.

Have the student hold a bar magnet vertically and suspend two paper clips from it, side by side with their upper ends against the end of the magnet, and observe what happens. Finally, have the student place a paper clip between the N end of one magnet and the S end of the other and slowly pull the magnets apart until the paper clip is disconnected from one of them. Ask the student to repeat the activity several times and observe from which magnet the paper clip disconnects.

COMMUNICATING

Materials
Communicating assessment sheet
a peanut in the shell
colored markers or pencils

Procedure
Tell the student to carefully examine the peanut in the shell. Then have the student follow the directions on the assessment sheet and communicate by drawing pictures to illustrate what a peanut looks like inside and outside.

ESTIMATING

Materials
Estimating assessment sheet
bag of plastic foam peanuts
4 containers of various sizes, 1 liter (such as a plastic soda bottle) and smaller, marked containers 1 through 4 (a permanent pen [such as a Sharpie™] can be used to number the objects)
2-liter plastic soda bottle filled with plastic foam peanuts and marked "Container 5"

Procedure
Explain to the student that the plastic foam peanuts and the containers will be used to help estimate the number of peanuts in the large plastic soda bottle. Suggest that the student may want to start by estimating the number of peanuts the smallest container will hold, count the peanuts to determine the accuracy of the estimate, and continue with the other containers. Have the student describe the technique he or she used for estimating.

MEASURING

Materials
Measuring assessment sheet
variety of 10 small objects (such as a paper clip)
balance
set of gram weights

Procedure
Tell the student to estimate the mass of each of the ten objects by placing an object in one hand and gram weights in the other until the two hands feel the same. Have the student record the name of the object and the estimate of its mass. Then have the student use the balance to determine the actual mass in grams of each object. Have the student answer the questions on the assessment sheet.

COLLECTING DATA

Materials
Collecting Data assessment sheet
10 green beans
plastic knife
colored markers or pencils

Procedure
Ask the student to open each green bean, count the number of seeds, and record the number of seeds in the chart. Then have the student use the data collected to construct a histogram of the number of seeds in green beans by coloring the squares corresponding to the number of seeds indicated below the chart.

CLASSIFYING

Materials
Classifying assessment sheet
variety of seeds in a reclosable plastic bag
colored markers or pencils

Procedure
Have the student sort the seeds into two groups by placing them in the boxes. Ask the student to trace around the seeds and color them. Then have the student label each of the groups and describe how the seeds in each group are alike. Ask the student to sort the seeds into two groups in a different way. Have the student trace around the seeds and color them. Ask the student to label each of these groups. Then have the student describe how the seeds in each group are different.

INFERRING

Materials
Inferring assessment sheet
6 pieces of fabric with different textures
    (5 cm × 5 cm)
Mystery Rubbing (made by gently rubbing
    with a crayon on a piece of paper placed
    over one of the pieces of fabric)
crayon

Procedure
Explain how to make a rubbing of a fabric by placing one piece of fabric under one of the circles on the assessment sheet and rubbing gently with the crayon. Have the student make rubbings of the other fabrics. Then ask the student to observe each of the rubbings and infer which piece of fabric was used to make the Mystery Rubbing.

PREDICTING

Materials
Predicting assessment sheet
100-ml graduated cylinder filled with
    20-ml of water
25 marbles

Procedure
Explain that the student will construct a graph showing the water level in the 100-ml graduated cylinder as marbles are added and will use the graph to make predictions. Ask each student to record the water level before any marbles are added. Then have each student add five marbles, record the water level, and make a bar on the graph to show the water level with five marbles added. Ask each student to add 10 more marbles for a total of 15 marbles, record the water level, and make a bar on the graph to show the water level with 15 marbles added.

Have each student predict what the water level will be with 10 marbles added, 20 marbles, and 25 marbles. Ask the student to test these predictions by actually adding the marbles and recording the water level, and to use this information to complete the bar graph.

MAKING MODELS

Materials
Making Models assessment sheet
10 cotton balls
white glue

Procedure
Have the student model the various cloud types at different levels in the atmosphere by

pulling and shaping the cotton balls. Have the student glue the cotton to the "Types of Clouds" chart.

INTERPRETING DATA

Materials
Interpreting Data assessment sheet
red, blue, and yellow watercolors

Procedure
Explain to the student that only the three watercolors can be used to make the color wheel. Tell the student that red, blue, and yellow are the primary colors and that the other colors, which are called secondary colors, can be made by mixing the primary colors. Ask the student to complete the color wheel, record which primary colors were mixed to obtain the secondary colors, and to give an interpretation of why the color wheel is arranged as it is.

MAKING GRAPHS

Materials
Making Graphs assessment sheet
self-stick dot for each student
metric tape measure at least 18-decimeters in length (or, two 10-decimeter tape measures) attached to a wall, extending from the floor upward with zero at the floor level (or, use masking tape marked in decimeters)

Procedure
Have each student go to the measuring tape with a partner. Have each place a self-stick dot on the decimeter mark nearest to the partner's height. When all students have placed their dots on the measuring tape, tally the heights of the students. The tally might look something like this:

Height in Decimeters	10	11	12	13	14	15	16
Number of Students	—	2	12	10	4	1	—

Tell each student to graph these data on the assessment sheet. Tell students to title the graph and to use numerals on each row to indicate the numbers of students.

HYPOTHESIZING

Materials
Hypothesizing assessment sheet
250-ml graduated cylinder filled with water
water
4 sponges of the same thickness cut to the following sizes: 2 cm × 2 cm, 3 cm × 3 cm, 4 cm × 4 cm, and 5 cm × 5 cm
construction paper

Procedure
Explain that hypotheses are educated guesses about the answer to a question. Tell each student to give a hypothesis (educated guess) to answer the following question: How does the size of a sponge affect the amount of water it will hold?

Tell each student to test the hypothesis by placing each sponge on a sheet of construction paper and pouring water from the graduated cylinder evenly over the sponge until the water leaks out of the sponge and onto the paper. Tell the student to add water a little at a time and to check for water on the paper after each addition. Ask the student to record how much water was needed to saturate each sponge by subtracting the amount of water left in the cylinder from 250. Then have the student compare the hypothesis to the actual results and tell whether or not the hypothesis was correct.

CONTROLLING VARIABLES

Materials
Controlling Variables assessment sheet
rug or blanket to cover table
12-inch ruler with grove down the center
marble
metric tape measure or meter stick
6 books or blocks of the same thickness (about 1 cm each)

Procedure
Cover the table top with a rug or blanket to provide friction to decrease the distance the marble will roll. Explain that the student will change the height of a ramp to determine whether ramp height affects the distance a marble rolls when it is released from the top of the ramp. Demonstrate how to set the ruler on one of the books or blocks to make a ramp and how to roll the marble down the groove in the middle of the ruler. Tell the student to measure the distance the marble travels from the end of the ramp in centimeters. Ask the student to record the measurement.

Have the student add a book or block to increase the height of the ramp, measure the distance the marble travels, and record the distance. Have the student continue to raise the ramp, roll the marble down the ramp, and measure the distance it travels until the ramp is 6 books or blocks in height. Have the student record which variable was changed, which responded to the change, and which were kept constant.

DEFINING OPERATIONALLY

Materials
Defining Operationally assessment sheet
iodine (diluted with water)
potato
bread
pasta
crackers

Procedure
Explain that potatoes, bread, pasta, and crackers are carbohydrates, which have nutrients that give the body quick energy. Carbohydrates include foods that have sugar and starches. Explain that if the drop of iodine turns blue-black, the food contains starch. Tell the student to place a drop of iodine on each of the foods to determine which foods contains starch. Ask the student to use what they learned in this activity to give a definition of carbohydrates.

INVESTIGATING
Materials
Investigating assessment sheet
vinegar
eye dropper
plastic wrap or waxed paper
baking soda and 3 different white powders
    (e.g., cornstarch, sugar, salt) numbered
    1, 2, 3, and 4. Place one teaspoon of each
    of the white powders on the plastic wrap
    or waxed paper.

Procedure
Explain that the student will design an investigation to solve a problem. The problem is to determine which of the white powers is baking soda. Tell the students that baking soda will fizz when it comes into contact with an acid such as vinegar. Explain that there are many ways to solve the problem, but that the student must set up a "fair" test for all the white powders. Have the student describe what will be done and construct a chart to show the results.

OBSERVING

1. What happens when you touch one end of the bar magnet to a paper clip?

   _____

2. Put the magnet on the table. What happens when you touch one end of a paper clip to several places along the sides and at the ends of the magnet?

   _____

   _____

   _____

3. Put the magnet on the table. What happens when you slide another magnet toward it so that the N (north) ends of the magnets approach each other?

   _____

   _____

4. Put the magnet on the table. What happens when you slide another magnet toward it so that the N and S (south) ends of the magnets approach each other?

   _____

   _____

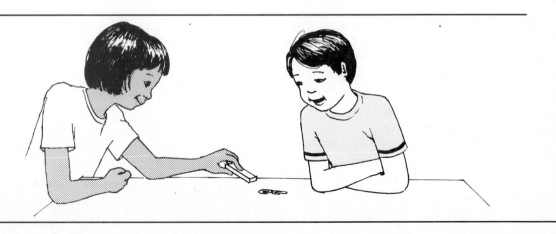

5. Hold the bar magnet in a vertical position and suspend two paper clips from the lower end of the magnet so that the paper clips are side by side with their upper ends against the end of the magnet. What happens to the paper clips?

_____

_____

_____

6. Put two bar magnets on the table with their N and S ends together. Pull the magnets apart and place a paper clip between the ends. Slowly pull the magnets apart until the paper clip is disconnected from one of them. Repeat several times. Does the paper clip disconnect from the both magnets or does it disconnect more often from one magnet?

_____

_____

_____

1. Examine the peanut closely. In the box, trace around the peanut and draw lines to show the shell's pattern.

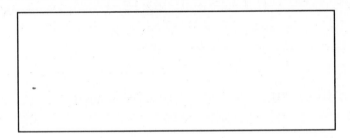

2. Gently break the shell of the peanut and separate the two halves. Draw the inside of the peanut shell in the box.

3. Gently break apart one peanut and separate the two halves. Draw the inside of the peanut in the box below.

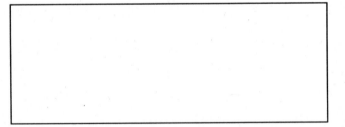

4. Look closely at all the parts of the peanut. List the things that are special about this peanut.

_____

_____

ESTIMATING

1. Use the plastic foam peanuts and containers 1 through 4 to help estimate the number of peanuts in the soda bottle (container 5).

2. Estimate and then count the number of peanuts that each container holds.

Container	Estimate	Actual Number
Container 1		
Container 2		
Container 3		
Container 4		

3. Describe what you did to estimate.

_____

_____

_____

4. Estimate how many peanuts are in container 5.

_____

5. Describe what you did to estimate.

_____

_____

_____

MEASURING

1. Hold an object in one hand and gram weights in the other hand.

2. Estimate the mass of each object in grams.

3. Place the object on one side of the balance and gram weights on the other side to find out the actual mass of the object in grams.

4. Record these data in the chart.

Object	Estimated Mass in Grams	Actual Mass in Grams

5. Which object has the most mass? _____

6. Which object has the least mass? _____

COLLECTING DATA

1. Open ten green beans and count the seeds.

2. Record the number of seeds you find in each bean.

Beans	1	2	3	4	5	6	7	8	9	10
Number of Seeds										

3. Color one square below for each bean that had
    3 seeds. Do the same for 4 seeds, 5 seeds, 6 seeds,
    7 seeds, 8 seeds, and 9 seeds.

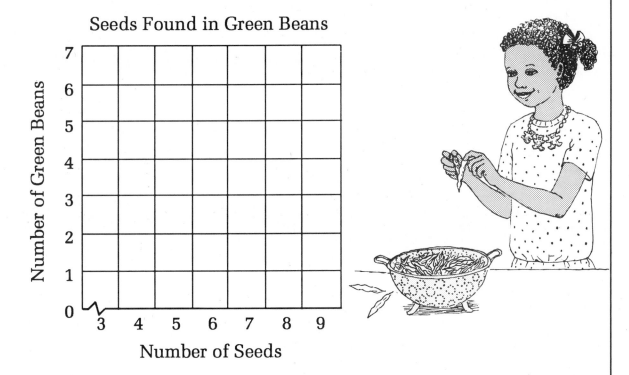

Seeds Found in Green Beans

4. What is the most common number of seeds found
    in a green bean? _____

Name _____

CLASSIFYING

1. Sort the seeds into two groups in the boxes below.

2. Trace around the seeds and color them. Label each group.

Label _____   Label _____

3. How are the seeds in each group alike?

_____

4. Sort the seeds a different way in the boxes below.

5. Trace around the seeds and color them. Label each group.

Label _____   Label _____

6. How are the seeds in each group different?

_____

36

Level 3

INFERRING

1. Make a rubbing of each fabric by placing it under one of the circles and gently rubbing a crayon on the circle.

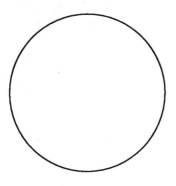
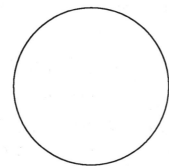
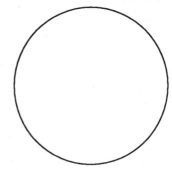

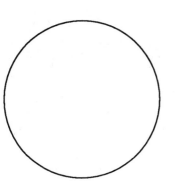
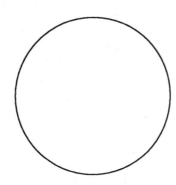
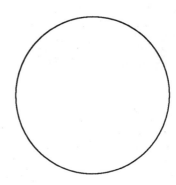

2. Circle the rubbing of the fabric that was used to make the Mystery Rubbing.

3. What helped you identify the fabric that was used to make the Mystery Rubbing?

_____

_____

_____

PREDICTING

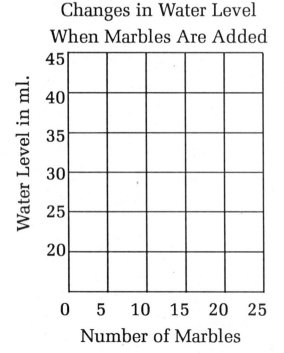

1. Pour 20 ml of water into the graduated cylinder.

2. Record the water level in the chart and on the graph.

3. Drop five marbles in the cylinder and record the water level in the chart and on the graph.

4. Add 10 more marbles so you have 15 marbles in the cylinder. Record the water level below.

5. Predict what the water level will be with 10 marbles. _____ ml

6. Predict what the water level will be with 20 marbles. _____ ml

7. Predict what the water level will be with 25 marbles. _____ ml

8. Test each of your predictions with the marbles and the cylinder.

9. Record the actual water level in the chart and on the graph.

Number of Marbles	Water Level in ml.
0	
5	
15	
10	
20	
25	

Changes in Water Level When Marbles Are Added

Water Level in ml.

45
40
35
30
25
20

0   5   10   15   20   25

Number of Marbles

Name

MAKING MODELS

1. Shape the cotton balls to resemble each type of cloud.

2. Glue the cotton to the cloud chart.

Types of Clouds   20,000 meters

Feathery Clouds

15,000 meters

Storm Clouds

10,000 meters

Fluffy
Clouds

5,000 meters

Layered Clouds

Fog   Ground level

INTERPRETING DATA

1. Use only red, blue, and yellow watercolors to make the color wheel below.

2. You may mix the primary colors (red, blue, and yellow) to make the secondary colors (purple, green, and orange).

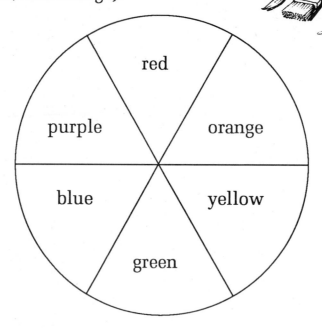

3. Which colors did you mix to make orange? _____

4. Which colors did you mix to make green? _____

5. Which colors did you mix to make purple? _____

6. Why do you think the colors are arranged this way on the color wheel?

_____

_____

_____

MAKING GRAPHS

1. Go to the measuring tape with your partner.

2. Have your partner place the dot on the decimeter mark nearest to your height.

3. When everyone has placed a dot on the measuring tape, complete the chart and the graph below.

Height in Decimeters	10	11	12	13	14	15	16	17
Number of Students								

Title _____

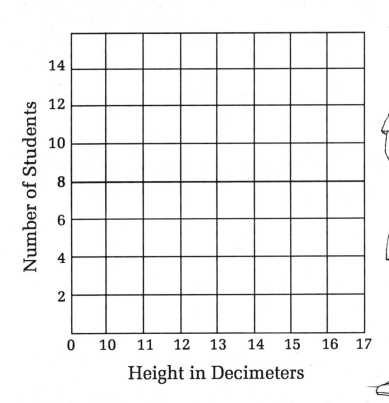

4. What is the most common height of students in your class? _____

Name _____

HYPOTHESIZING

1. **Question:** How does the size of a sponge affect the amount of water it will hold? Your hypothesis (educated guess):

   _____

   _____

2. Place the 2 cm × 2 cm sponge on the construction paper.
   - Fill the graduated cylinder with water to the 250-ml mark.
   - Pour water 10 ml at a time evenly over the sponge. Each time, lift the sponge. When the paper is wet, stop pouring.
   - Subtract the amount of water left in the cylinder from 250 to find out how much water saturated the sponge.
   - Record this number in the chart below.
   - Refill the graduated cylinder.

3. Repeat with the remaining three sponges.

    Sponge Size   250 ml – ____ (water level after saturating sponge) = ____ ml

Sponge Size		
2 cm × 2 cm		
3 cm × 3 cm		
4 cm × 4 cm		
5 cm × 5 cm		

4. Did your investigation support your hypothesis? _____

5. Explain. _____

   _____

   _____

CONTROLLING VARIABLES

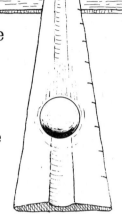

1. Make a ramp by setting the ruler on top of one of the books or blocks.

2. Roll the marble from the top of the ramp and measure the distance it travels from the end of the ramp.

3. Record the distance in the chart below.

4. Add another book and roll the marble again. Measure the distance it travels from the end of the ramp.

5. Repeat this procedure until the ramp is 6 books high.

Height of Ramp	Distance marble travels from end of ramp in centimeters
1 book	
2 books	
3 books	
4 books	
5 books	
6 books	

6. Which variable did you change?

_____

7. Which variable responded to the change (what did you measure)?

_____

8. Which variables were kept constant?

_____

DEFINING OPERATIONALLY

1. Carbohydrates give your body quick energy.
   - Carbohydrates include foods that have sugar and starches.
   - Iodine will turn blue-black when placed on something that contains starch.

2. Place a drop of iodine on each of the foods to test whether any of them contain starch.

3. In the chart below, record the color of the iodine on the food.

Food	Color of Iodine	Contains Starch (Yes or No)
potato		
bread		
pasta		
cracker		

4. Give your definition of a carbohydrate based on what you did in this activity.

_____

_____

_____

INVESTIGATING

1. **Problem:** Which of these white powders is baking soda? Design and conduct an investigation to help you find out. *Note: Baking soda will fizz when it comes into contact with an acid such as vinegar.*

2. Describe what you will do to find out which white powder is baking soda.

_____

_____

3. Construct a chart to show your results.

Powder	Reaction with Vinegar

4. **Conclusion:** Which of these white powders is baking soda?

_____

5. What did you learn from this investigation?

_____

_____

_____

OBSERVING

Materials
Observing assessment sheet
a shell
colored markers or pencils

Procedure
Have the student observe the shell using the senses of sight, hearing, smell, and touch. Ask the student to describe the shell's color, shape, size, texture, sound, and odor. Tell the student to record the observations. Have the student draw and color a picture of the shell.

COMMUNICATING

Materials
Communicating assessment sheet
a container or label from food or other household product *(Note: It might be interesting for students to read the contents of "junk" foods.)*

Procedure
Tell the student to read and record the ingredients listed on the label. Explain that ingredients are listed in order of abundance. Then have the student tell what the label communicates about the product.

ESTIMATING

Materials
Estimating assessment sheet
small box of raisin cereal
shirt box lid with a grid glued or drawn in the bottom
various small containers

Procedure
Explain to the student that the containers and the grid in the box lid can be used to help estimate the number of raisins in the box of cereal. (If students have difficulty getting started, you may want to suggest that the student start by pouring the cereal into the box lid and shaking the cereal so it is evenly distributed on the grid.) Ask the student how the total number of raisins in the box could be estimated without counting each one. (The student could count the raisins in one of the squares in the grid and multiply by the total number of squares. Another method would be to count the raisins in one container filled with cereal and multiply by the number of containers the box holds. Or, the student might pour the cereal into a pile, half the pile, half the pile again and again, then count the raisins in a small pile and multiply it by as many 2s together as the number of times the pile was halved.)

Allow the student to use any technique for sampling and estimating the number of raisins in the box. Have the student describe the technique used for estimating.

MEASURING

Materials
Measuring assessment sheet
metric tape measure

Procedure
Have each student estimate the length of the body parts listed on the assessment sheet by ordering them from shortest to longest. Tell the student to determine the length of his or her body parts with the metric tape measure. Have the student record the lengths and order the body parts from shortest to longest. Then have the student compare the actual lengths of each body part with the estimated lengths.

COLLECTING DATA

Materials
Collecting Data assessment sheet
50 plastic or plastic-coated paper clips of

different colors in a sock (suggested set:
15 blue, 12 red, 10 green, 8 yellow, and
5 orange paper clips)
markers or pencils (in colors corresponding
to the colors of the paper clips)

Procedure

Ask the student to remove the paper clips
from the sock one at a time and record the
color of the paper clip in the chart using tally
marks. Then have the student color in one
square on the graph paper, starting from the
bottom, to represent the color of each paper
clip. Explain that a new column should be
started for a different paper clip color. Then
have the student answer the questions on the
assessment sheet.

CLASSIFYING

Materials
Classifying assessment sheet
20 different screws and bolts
colored markers or pencils

Procedure
Have the student sort the screws and bolts into
two groups by placing them in the circles. Ask
the student to trace around the screws and
bolts and color them. Then have the student
label each of the groups and describe how the
items in each group are alike. Ask the student
to sort the screws and bolts into two groups in
a different way. Have the student trace around
the screws and bolts and color them. Ask the
student to label each of these groups. Then
have the student describe how the items in
each group are different.

INFERRING

Materials
Inferring assessment sheet
magazine advertisement

Procedure
Ask the student to list an observation about
the advertisement and an inference that

could be made from the observation. Give an
example; e.g., *observation:* the girl in the
advertisement is petting a cat; *inference:* the
cat is purring. Explain that observations can
be verified by looking at the advertisement
but inferences require evaluation and
judgement based on past experiences and
cannot be verified by looking at the
advertisement. Have the student record
observations and inferences and answer the
question on the assessment sheet.

PREDICTING

Materials
Predicting assessment sheet
penny

Procedure
Explain that the penny will be flipped 40
times and the student will record whether the
coin lands on heads or tails. Then the student
will use the results of the 40 coin flips to
predict what will happen if the coin is
flipped 10 more times. Ask each student to
test the prediction by flipping the coin 10
more times and recording the result.

MAKING MODELS

Materials
Making Models assessment sheet
black and orange crayons or markers
scissors
white glue

Procedure
Have the student outline the teeth with the
black crayon or marker and color the gums
orange. Tell the student to carefully cut out
the shape on the solid lines, and then fold it
along the dotted lines and glue it together.
Have the student answer the questions on the
assessment sheet.

INTERPRETING DATA

Materials
Interpreting Data assessment sheet
calculator

Procedure
Explain to the student that the calculator can be used to answer the questions about the active volcanoes of North America. Have the student look at the table of information about active volcanoes in North America and answer the questions on the assessment sheet.

MAKING GRAPHS

Materials
Making Graphs assessment sheet
metric ruler

Procedure
Students will work in pairs. Explain that one person will hold the metric ruler at the 33-cm end. The other person will hold a thumb and forefinger at the zero end of the ruler, without actually touching it. This person should be prepared to grab the ruler when the partner releases it. The person holding the ruler releases it 10 times, and the person grabbing the ruler records how far from the zero end it was grasped.

Explain that both students will graph these data. Tell them to title the graph, use numerals on each column to indicate the trial number, and use numerals on each row to indicate the distance from zero that the ruler was grasped.

HYPOTHESIZING

Materials
Hypothesizing assessment sheet
6 straws
scissors

Procedure
Demonstrate how to cut one end of the straw to form a point and how to blow into the pointed end to produce a sound. Explain that hypotheses are educated guesses about the answer to a question. Tell each student to give a hypothesis (educated guess) to answer the following question: How does the length of the straw affect the pitch of the sound produced?

Have the student test the hypothesis by cutting each straw to a different length and observing the pitch of the sound produced. Have students place the straws in order from the highest to the lowest pitch and tape the straws to the assessment sheet. Then have the student compare the hypothesis to the results of the activity and tell whether or not the hypothesis was correct.

CONTROLLING VARIABLES

Materials
Controlling Variables assessment sheet
6 pieces of string (10 cm, 20 cm, 30 cm, 40 cm, 50 cm, and 60 cm in length)
6 washers (one tied to the end of each string)
pencil
tape
timer

Procedure
Explain to the student that counting the number of times the pendulum swings in 15 seconds will help determine if the length of the pendulum makes a difference in the number of times it swings. Demonstrate how to tape the pencil to the edge of the table, hang the pendulum on the pencil, and start the pendulum in motion by pulling it up to the level of the table and releasing it. Start the timer at the same instant the pendulum is released. Tell the student to count the number of times each pendulum swings back and forth in 15 seconds. Ask the student to record the length of each pendulum and the number of swings for each pendulum and answer the questions about the investigation.

DEFINING OPERATIONALLY

Materials
Defining Operationally assessment sheet
flashlight bulb
"D" dry cell
insulated wire
science book or dictionary

Procedure
Explain that the flashlight bulb, "D" dry cell, and insulated wire can be connected to make a complete circuit in which the bulb lights. Have the student construct a complete circuit by following the diagram. Ask the student to use what was learned in this activity to give a definition of a circuit. Then have the student look up the definition of *circuit* in a science book or the dictionary and compare it to his or her own definition.

INVESTIGATING

Materials
Investigating assessment sheet
meter stick
4 different kinds of balls (e.g., tennis ball, golf ball, rubber ball, super ball)

Procedure
Explain that each student will design an investigation to solve a problem. The problem is to determine which ball bounces the highest. Explain that there are many ways to solve the problem, but that the student must set up a "fair" test for all the balls.

Name _____

OBSERVING

1. Use your eyes, ears, hands, and nose to observe the shell.

2. Describe the color of the shell. _____

   _____

3. Describe the shape of the shell. _____

   _____

4. Describe the size of the shell. _____

   _____

5. Describe the texture of the shell. _____

   _____

6. Describe the sound of the shell. _____

   _____

7. Describe the odor of the shell. _____

   _____

8. Draw and color a picture of the shell in the box below.

Name

COMMUNICATING

Read the ingredients listed on the product label. List the ingredients in order and the amount of each ingredient (if given) in the chart below. (Ingredients on product labels are listed from most to least abundance.)

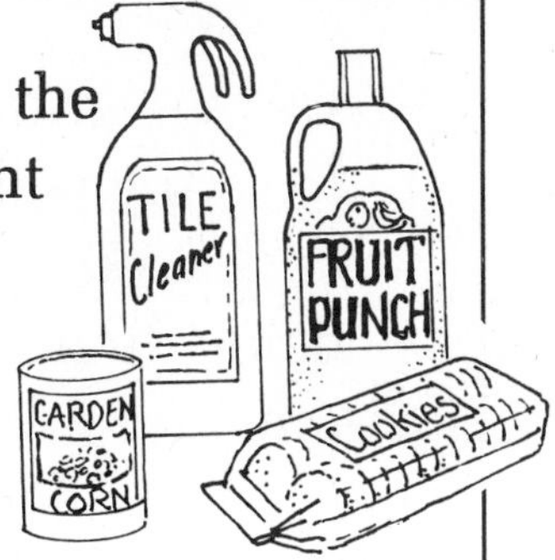

Name of Product ______________________

Ingredient	Amount of Ingredient (if given)

3. List everything you learned about this product from the label.

____

____

____

ESTIMATING

1. Use the grid in the box and/or the containers to estimate the number of raisins in the box of cereal. (Do not count every raisin.) Use the box below to do your calculations.

2. Record your estimate of the number of raisins in the box. _____

3. Describe what you did to estimate the number of raisins in the box.

    _____

    _____

    _____

    _____

MEASURING

1. Estimate the length of each of your body parts by putting them in order from shortest to longest: the length of the thumb, hand, foot, arm, and leg; the distance around the knee, head, neck, wrist, and ankle.

Body Part	Estimated Order 1=shortest 10=longest	Measurement	Actual Order 1=shortest 10=longest

2. Use the metric tape measure to measure your body parts and write the actual measurements in centimeters.

3. Use the actual measurements to order your body parts from shortest to longest, using 1 for the shortest and 10 for the longest.

4. Compare your estimates with your measurements.
How close was your estimated order to the actual order?

_____

_____

5. What surprised you?

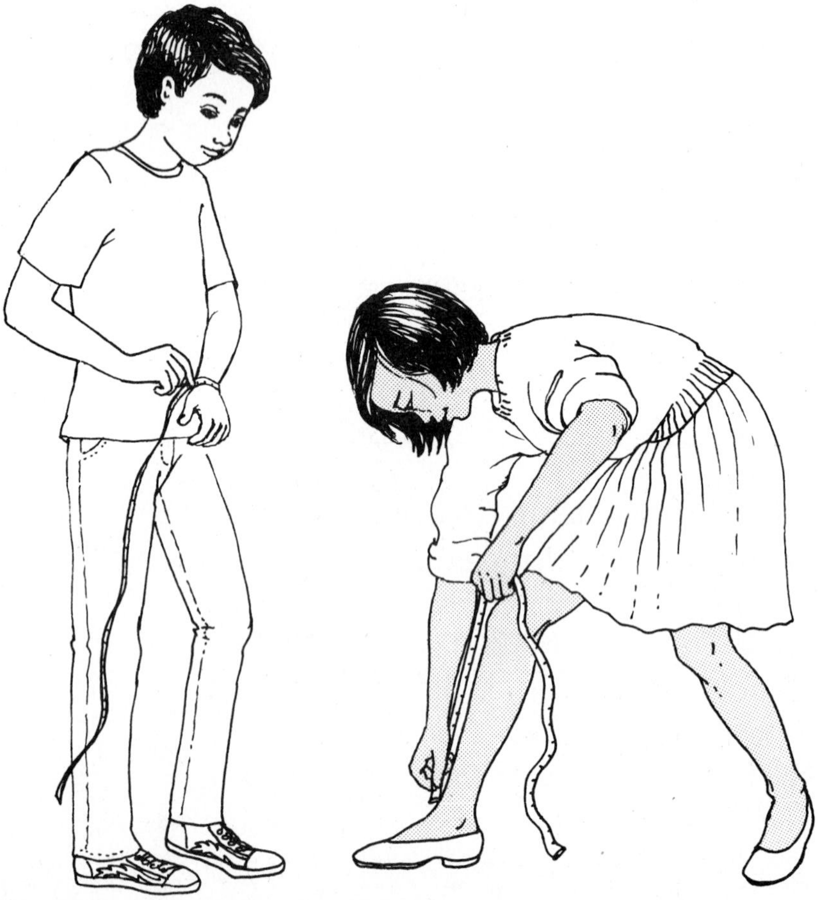

_____

_____

_____

_____

_____

COLLECTING DATA

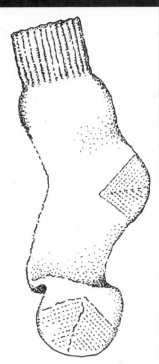

1. Reach into the sock and remove one paper clip.

2. List the color of the paper clip and put a tally mark in the chart.

3. Remove another paper clip. If the color is different from the first color, list the color in the chart and make a tally mark next to it. If the color is the same as the first color, put another tally mark next to the first color.

4. Continue taking paper clips out of the sock and recording their colors in the chart.

Paper Clips

Color	Tally Marks	Total

5. Fill in the graph on the next page. Color one box for each paper clip. The box should be the same color as the paper clip. Start at the bottom of the graph and use a different color for the boxes in each column. Columns should show how many paper clips you have of each color.

15				
14				
13				
12				
11				
10				
9				
8				
7				
6				
5				
4				
3				
2				
1				

_____	_____	_____	_____	_____
color	color	color	color	color

6. Which color were the greatest number of paper clips?_____

7. Which color were the least number of paper clips? _____

CLASSIFYING

1. Sort the screws and bolts into two groups in the circles below.

2. Trace around the screws and bolts and color them.

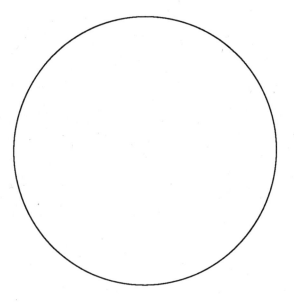 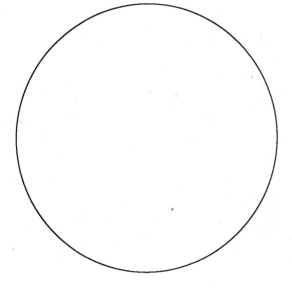

Label _____   Label _____

3. How are the items in each group alike?

_____

_____

_____

4. Sort the screws and bolts a different way into two groups in the circles below.

5. Trace around the screws and bolts and color them.

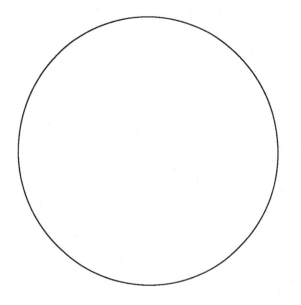 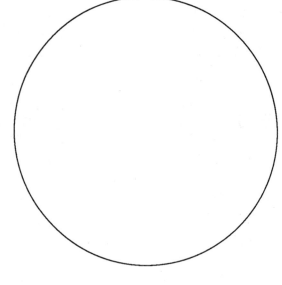

Label _____   Label _____

6. How are the items in each group different?

_____

_____

_____

INFERRING

1. Look at the advertisement. List an observation and an inference that could be made about the advertisement in the chart below. An example is given for you.

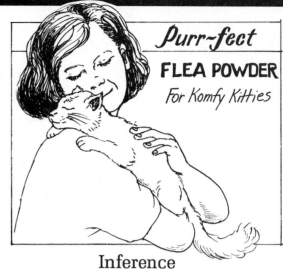

Purr~fect
FLEA POWDER
For Komfy Kitties

Observation	Inference
The girl is petting the cat.	The cat is purring.

2. What do you think the advertisers want you to believe will happen if you use their product?

_____

_____

Name

PREDICTING

1. Flip the penny 40 times and record in the chart below whether it lands on heads or tails.

Trial No.	1	2	3	4	5	6	7	8	9	10
H or T										

Trial No.	11	12	13	14	15	16	17	18	19	20
H or T										

Trial No.	21	22	23	24	25	26	27	28	29	30
H or T										

Trial No.	31	32	33	34	35	36	37	38	39	40
H or T										

2. How many times did the penny land on heads? _____

3. How many times did the penny land on tails? _____

4. Predict how many times the penny would land on heads and how many times on tails if you flipped it 10 more times.

heads _____

tails _____

5. Flip the penny 10 more times and record the results in the chart below.

Trial No.	1	2	3	4	5	6	7	8	9	10
H or T										

6. How many times did the penny land on heads? _____

7. How many times did the penny land on tails? _____

8. Explain why your prediction might not match the actual number of heads and tails.

_____

_____

MAKING MODELS

1. Outline the teeth in black. Color the gums orange.

2. Cut out the shape on the solid lines. Fold along the dotted lines. Follow the directions for overlapping and gluing the model.

3. How is this model the same as real teeth?

   _____

4. How is this model different from real teeth?

   _____

Name

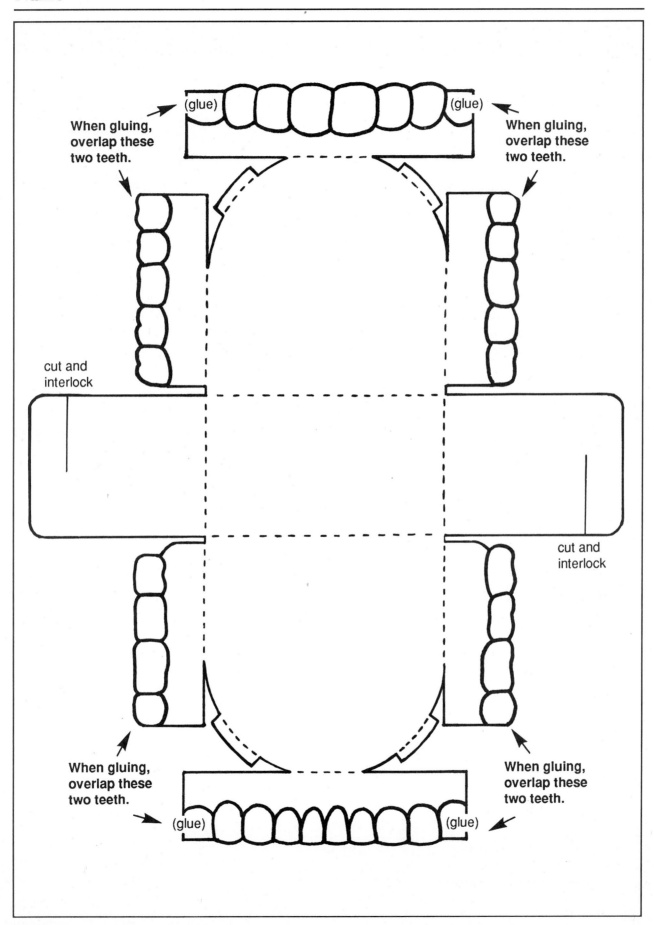

When gluing, overlap these two teeth.

(glue)   (glue)

When gluing, overlap these two teeth.

cut and interlock

cut and interlock

When gluing, overlap these two teeth.

When gluing, overlap these two teeth.

(glue)   (glue)

INTERPRETING DATA

1. Read the table below and answer the questions about the information.

Active Volcanoes of North America

Name (year of latest activity)	Location	Height (in meters)
Colima (1986)	Mexico	4,268
Redoubt (1966)	Alaska	3,108
Iliamna (1978)	Alaska	3,076
Mount St. Helens (1986)	Washington	2,950
Shishaldin (1981)	Aleutian Islands	2,861
Veniaminof (1884)	Alaska	2,507
Pavlof (1984)	Aleutian Islands	2,504
El Chichon (1983)	Mexico	2,225
Makushin (1980)	Aleutian Islands	2,036
Trident (1963)	Alaska	1,832
Great Sitkan (1974)	Aleutian Islands	1,740
Akutan (1980)	Aleutian Islands	1,303
Kiska (1969)	Aleutian Islands	1,303
Sequam (1977)	Alaska	1,054

2. How high is the highest active volcano? _____

3. How high is the lowest active volcano? _____

4. What is the difference in height between the highest and lowest volcano? _____

5. What is the most recent date of volcanic activity? _____

6. What is the least recent date of volcanic activity? _____

7. How many years passed between the most recent activity and the least recent activity? _____

MAKING GRAPHS

1. Work with a partner. One person will hold the centimeter ruler at the 33-cm end. The other person will hold a thumb and index finger at the zero end of the ruler without actually touching it.

2. The person holding the ruler will drop it and the other person will try to catch it as close to the 0-cm mark as possible. Record the cm mark at which the ruler is caught.

3. Repeat for a total of 10 trials.

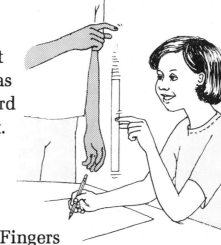

Response Time

Trial Number	Place (cm) Where Fingers Caught Falling Ruler
1	
2	
3	
4	
5	
6	
7	
8	
9	
10	

4. Graph the results of this activity. Remember to title your graph, use numerals on each column to indicate the trial number, and use numerals on each row to indicate the distance from 0 that the ruler was caught.

Title _____

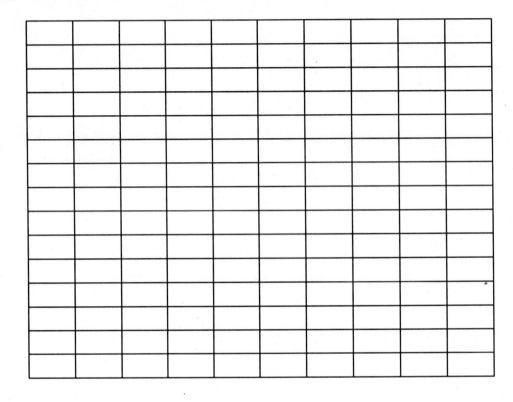

_____

5. Which trial had the shortest reaction time? _____

6. Did reaction time improve with practice? _____

HYPOTHESIZING

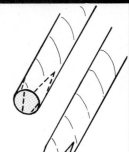

1. Cut one end of one of the straws to form a point and blow into this end of the straw to produce a sound. Observe the pitch of the sound produced (high or low).

2. **Question:** How does the length of the straw affect the pitch of the sound produced?

   Your hypothesis (educated guess): _____

   _____

   _____

3. Trim the five remaining straws to different lengths. Then cut one end of each straw, blow into this end, and observe the pitch of the sound produced.

4. Arrange your six straws in order from the highest to the lowest pitch and tape the straws in the box below.

Highest

↑
¦
¦
¦
¦
¦
¦
¦
↓

Lowest

5. Did your investigation prove your hypothesis is correct? _____

CONTROLLING VARIABLES

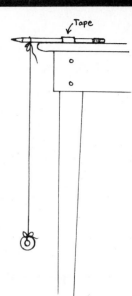

1. Tape the pencil to the table so that it hangs over the edge. Hang the longest pendulum from the pencil. Hold the pendulum even with the top of the table and release it.

2. Count how many times it swings back and forth in 15 seconds and record the number of swings in the chart below. Use the metric tape measure to measure the length of the pendulum. Repeat this procedure with the other five pendulums.

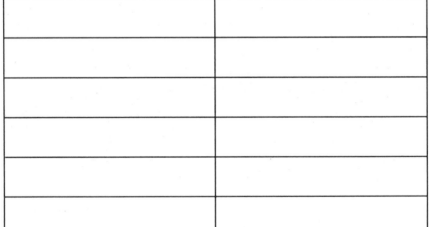

Length of Pendulum in cm	Number of Swings Back and Forth in 15 Seconds

3. Which variable did you change? _____

4. Which variable responded to the change (what did you count)?

    _____

5. Which variables were kept constant? _____

6. How does the length of the pendulum affect the number of times it swings in 15 seconds?_____

    _____

DEFINING OPERATIONALLY

1. Look at the diagram of the complete circuit. Set up the bulb, dry cell, and wire to make a complete circuit so the bulb lights.

2. Give your definition of a complete circuit based on what you did.

    _____

    _____

3. Look up *circuit* in your science book or the dictionary and write the definition given in the book.

    _____

    _____

4. How is your definition of a circuit different from the definition given in the book?

    _____

    _____

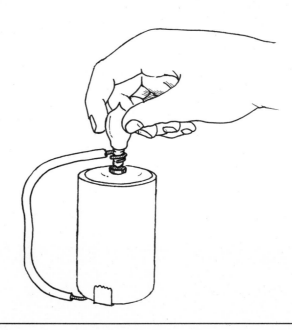

INVESTIGATING

1. **Problem:** Which of these balls bounces the highest? Design and conduct an investigation to find out.

2. Describe what you will do to determine which ball bounces the highest. _____

   _____

   _____

3. Construct a chart to show your results.

Type of ball	Trial 1	Trial 2	Trial 3	Average

4. Graph the results listed in your chart.

Title _____

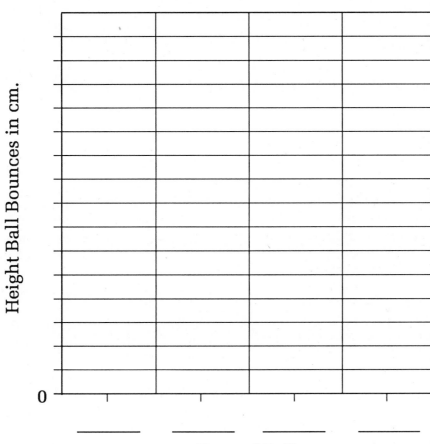

Height Ball Bounces in cm.

0

_____   _____   _____   _____

Type of Ball

5. **Conclusion:** Which of these balls bounces the highest?

_____

6. What did you learn from this investigation?

_____

_____

_____

LEVEL 5

OBSERVING

Materials
Observing assessment sheet
sugar cube
clear plastic cup filled with water
stirring stick
metric ruler

Procedure
Have the student observe the sugar cube using the senses of sight, hearing, smell, and touch. Ask the student to describe the sugar cube's shape, color, size, texture, sound, and odor. Tell the student that the metric ruler can be used to determine the length, width, and height of the sugar cube. Explain that the cup of water can be used to determine whether or not the sugar cube will dissolve in water. Ask the student to record observations.

COMMUNICATING

Materials
Communicating assessment sheet
a book about vertebrates
colored markers or pencils

Procedure
Tell the student to use the book to locate information about the five groups of vertebrates: fish, amphibians, reptiles, birds, and mammals. Have the student complete the table by listing features of each group of vertebrates, and by drawing one member of each group.

ESTIMATING

Materials
Estimating assessment sheet
pint jar filled with dry peas
pint jar filled with rice
pint jar filled with macaroni

box lid with grid drawn or glued to the inside bottom
several small containers

Procedure
Explain to the student that the grid box lid and containers can be used to help estimate the number of peas, rice, or macaroni pieces in each pint jar. (If the student has difficulty getting started, you may want to suggest that the student could start by pouring the pint jar of peas into the box lid and shaking the peas so they are evenly distributed on the grid.)

Ask the student how the total number of peas in the jar could be estimated without counting each one. (The student could count the peas in one of the squares in the grid and multiply by the total number of squares. Another method would be to count the peas one container holds and multiply by the number of containers the pint jar holds. Or, the student might pour the peas into a pile; separate one of those piles into two halves, and continue separating the pile into two halves until the peas are in a small pile; count the peas in this pile; and multiply by as many 2s as the number of times the pile was halved.)

Allow the student to use any technique for sampling and estimating the contents of the three pint jars. Then have the student describe the technique used for estimating the number of peas, rice, and macaroni pieces.

MEASURING

Materials
Measuring assessment sheet
graduated cylinder
water
variety of 10 small numbered objects that fit in the graduated cylinder (a permanent pen [such as a Sharpie™] can be used to number the objects)

Procedure

Have the student estimate the volume of the ten objects by placing them in order from least volume to greatest volume. Tell the student that the graduated cylinder will be used to determine the actual volume of each of the objects. Explain that the volumes can be determined by measuring the amount of water each object displaces. One milliliter (1 ml) of water displaced is equal to the volume of one cubic centimeter (1 cm^3). Have the student record the volume of each object. Then have the student compare the actual volumes of the different objects.

COLLECTING DATA

Materials

Collecting Data assessment sheet
100 squares (2 cm × 2 cm) of construction paper of different colors in a school box (suggested set of squares: 50 red, 20 blue, 15 green, 10 yellow, and 5 orange squares)
markers or pencils (in colors corresponding to the colors of the squares)

Procedure

Ask the student to take 100 squares from the box one at a time (without looking in the box) and record the color of the squares in the chart using tally marks. Then have the student color in one square on the graph paper, starting at the left, to represent each construction paper square. Explain that a new column should be started for a different square color and that the graph paper squares should be colored the same color as the construction paper squares. Then have the student answer the questions on the assessment sheet.

CLASSIFYING

Materials

Classifying assessment sheet
8 different nuts in the shell (suggested nuts include: walnut, almond, peanut, filbert, pecan, acorn, Brazil nut, pistachio)
colored markers or pencils

Procedure

Have the student place the eight nuts into the box at the top of the assessment sheet. Ask the student to trace around the nuts and color them. Then have the student divide the nuts into two groups in the two boxes below the box at the top and list in the boxes the property that was used to sort the nuts (color, size, shape, texture, etc.). Have the student trace around the nuts and color them.

Ask the student to sort the nuts in each box into two more groups. Have the student trace and color the nuts and list the property that was used to make the new groupings. Finally, have the student separate each of these groups so each nut is in a box by itself. Have the student trace and color the nuts and list the properties of each of these groups.

INFERRING

Materials

Inferring assessment sheet
shoebox with 10 numbered holes in a line in the cover (large enough for a straw)
modeling clay or plaster of Paris molded into hills and valleys in the bottom of the shoebox (hills and valleys should extend the width of the shoebox)
straw marked off in centimeters with a permanent pen (such as a Sharpie™)

Procedure

Ask the student to slide the straw into each of the numbered holes in the shoebox lid and observe how far the straw goes down. Have the student record observations. Then have the student infer what the bottom of the box looks like and draw a diagram to illustrate the shape of the bottom of the box. Have the student uncover the box and compare the drawing to the actual contour of the clay.

PREDICTING

Materials

Predicting assessment sheet
die

Procedure

Explain that the student will toss the die 60 times and record the number on top of the die after each toss. Then the student will use the results of the 60 tosses to predict what will happen if the die is tossed 30 more times. Ask each student to test the prediction by tossing the die 30 more times and recording the result. Have the student answer the questions on the assessment sheet.

MAKING MODELS

Materials
Making Models assessment sheet
10 long bolts
10 short bolts
15 wing nuts
15 hex nuts

Procedure
Explain that the nuts and bolts represent atoms and will be put together to represent molecules. Then formulas will be written for each molecule. Use the following symbols: long bolt—Lo, short bolt—Sh, wing nut—Wg, and hex nut—Hx. Have the student place a hex nut on a long bolt. Then have the student write the formula for this "molecule" (LoHx). Ask the student to continue to make molecules using different combinations of nuts and bolts, and to write the formula for each molecule. Ask how the formulas are similar to the formulas used by scientists for molecules and compounds.

INTERPRETING DATA

Materials
Interpreting Data assessment sheet
calculator

Procedure
Explain to the student that the calculator can be used to answer the questions about the snakes of the world. Have the student look at the graph of information about snakes and answer the questions on the assessment sheet.

MAKING GRAPHS

Materials
Making Graphs assessment sheet
50 cm. of rubber tubing (approximately ¼ in. diameter)
4 different sized beakers filled with water numbered 1 through 4
large container (larger than the largest beaker)
timer

Procedure
Demonstrate how to submerge the entire tube in the water and pinch one end closed. Pull that end out and down the side until it is below the bottom of the beaker. Release the pinched end over the large container and record the time required to empty the beaker. Have the student repeat the procedure for each beaker and record the time required to empty each beaker. Have the student construct a graph. Tell the student to title the graph, use numerals along the bottom to indicate the size of each beaker, and use numerals along the side to indicate the time required to empty each beaker.

HYPOTHESIZING

Materials
Hypothesizing assessment sheet
6 numbered objects (e.g., 2 different balls, 2 different cubes, a cylinder, an irregularly shaped object). A permanent pen (such as a Sharpie™) can be used to number the objects.
tall, clear cylinder filled with water (objects should fit into cylinder)
timer

Procedure
Explain that hypotheses are educated guesses about the answer to a question. Tell each student to give a hypothesis (educated guess) to answer the following question: How do the properties (size, shape, volume, density, and weight) of an object affect how fast it will fall through a liquid? Ask the student to estimate the order of the objects from longest to

shortest fall time. Then have each student test the hypothesis by dropping each object in the cylinder of water and recording the time it takes to reach the bottom. Have students record the order of the objects from the longest to the shortest fall time. Then have the student compare the hypothesis to the results of the activity and tell whether or not the hypothesis was correct.

CONTROLLING VARIABLES

Materials
Controlling Variables assessment sheet
salt
teaspoon
250-ml clear container filled with water
water
stirring stick
timer

Procedure
Have the student add 1 teaspoon (5 ml) of salt to the 250-ml container and stir until the salt dissolves. Ask the student to record the length of time it takes for the salt to disappear. Have the student repeat the procedure using 2 teaspoons, 3 teaspoons, 4 teaspoons, and 5 teaspoons of salt (start with fresh water each time) and record the length of time it takes for the salt to disappear. Then have the student answer the questions on the assessment sheet.

DEFINING OPERATIONALLY

Materials
Defining Operationally assessment sheet
3 plastic foam balls
pipe cleaners
colored paper
scissors
buttons
twist ties
straws
toothpicks
beads
sticks

craft glue (tacky glue)
science book or dictionary

Procedure
Explain that an insect has three body segments, six legs, and two antennas. Have the student study the diagram of the insect. Then have the student use the craft materials to construct a model of an insect. Ask the student to describe the insect she or he constructed in order to give his or her own definition of an insect. Then have the student look up the definition of an insect in a science book or the dictionary and compare the definition in the book with his or her own.

INVESTIGATING

Materials
Investigating assessment sheet
box of paper clips
4 different magnets (e.g., bar magnet, horseshoe magnet, circular magnet, cubic or rectangular magnet)

Procedure
Explain that the student will design an investigation to solve a problem. The problem is to determine which magnet is the strongest. If a student has difficulty getting started, suggest that each magnet could be placed in the box of paper clips to see how many the magnet is able to pick up. Explain that there are many ways to solve the problem, but a "fair" test must be set up for all the magnets.

OBSERVING

1. Observe the cube using the sense of sight. Describe the cube.

   Color: _____

   _____

   Shape: _____

   _____

2 . Use the metric ruler to make observations about size of the cube.

   Length: _____ Width: _____ Height: _____

3. Observe the cube using the sense of touch. Describe the cube.

   Texture: _____

   _____

4. Observe the cube using the sense of hearing. Drop the cube on the table.

   Sound: _____

   _____

5. Observe the cube using the sense of smell. Describe the cube.

   Odor: _____

   _____

6. Place the cube in the cup of water and stir. Record your observations.

   _____

COMMUNICATING

1. Use the book to find information about the five groups of vertebrates: fish, amphibians, reptiles, birds, and mammals.

2. Complete the table by listing features of each group of vertebrates and drawing one member of each group.

Vertebrates

Group	Features	Example
Fish		
Amphibians		
Reptiles		
Birds		
Mammals		

Name _____

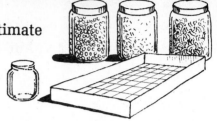

1. Use the grid in the box and/or the containers to estimate
   the number of items in each jar.

2. Use the boxes below to do your calculations.

Jar #1 Contents	Jar #2 Contents	Jar #3 Contents

3. Your estimates: Jar 1 _____

   Jar 2 _____

   Jar 3 _____

4. Describe what you did to estimate the number of items in each jar.

   Jar 1 _____

   _____

   _____

   Jar 2 _____

   _____

   _____

   Jar 3 _____

   _____

   _____

Name _____

MEASURING

1. Estimate the volume of each object by putting the objects in order from smallest volume to greatest volume. List the number on each object.

   Smallest ————————————————————————→ Greatest

2. Use the graduated cylinder to determine the volume of each object. Fill the cylinder halfway with water. Record the water level, before and after adding each object, in the chart below. The volume of the object is equal to one cubic centimeter (1 cm^3) for every milliliter (ml) displaced.

Actual Volume of Objects

Object Number	Water level with object – Beginning water level	Volume = __ ml = __ cm^3

3. Order the objects from smallest to greatest volume.

   Smallest ————————————————————————→ Greatest

COLLECTING DATA

1. Without looking in the box, take out one colored square. List the color of the square and put a tally mark in the chart.

2. Take out another square. If the color is different from the first color, list the color in the chart and make a tally mark next to it. If the color is the same, put another tally mark next to the first color.

3. Continue taking squares out of the box and recording the color in the chart until you have removed 100 squares.

Color	Tally Marks	Total

4. Fill in the graph below. Color boxes for each colored square, the same color as the square. Start at the bottom and use a different color for the boxes in each column. Each column should show how many squares you have of each color.

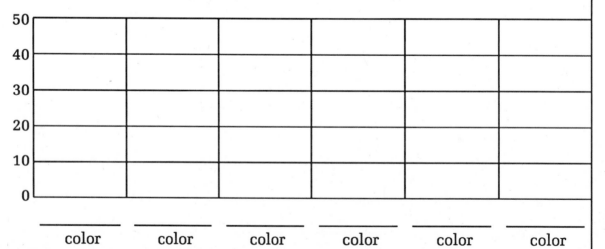

5. Of which color were the greatest number of squares? _____

   Of which color were the least number of squares? _____

CLASSIFYING

1. Place the eight nuts in the box at the top of the chart on the next page.

2. Trace around the nuts and color them.

3. Divide the nuts into two groups in the boxes below the large box at the top.

4. Trace around the nuts and color them. In the boxes, write the property you used to sort the nuts.

5. Group the nuts from each box into the two boxes below each box.

6. Trace around the nuts and color them. Write the property you used to sort the nuts.

7. Place one nut in each of the boxes at the bottom.

8. Trace around each nut and color it. In the boxes, write the properties of each nut.

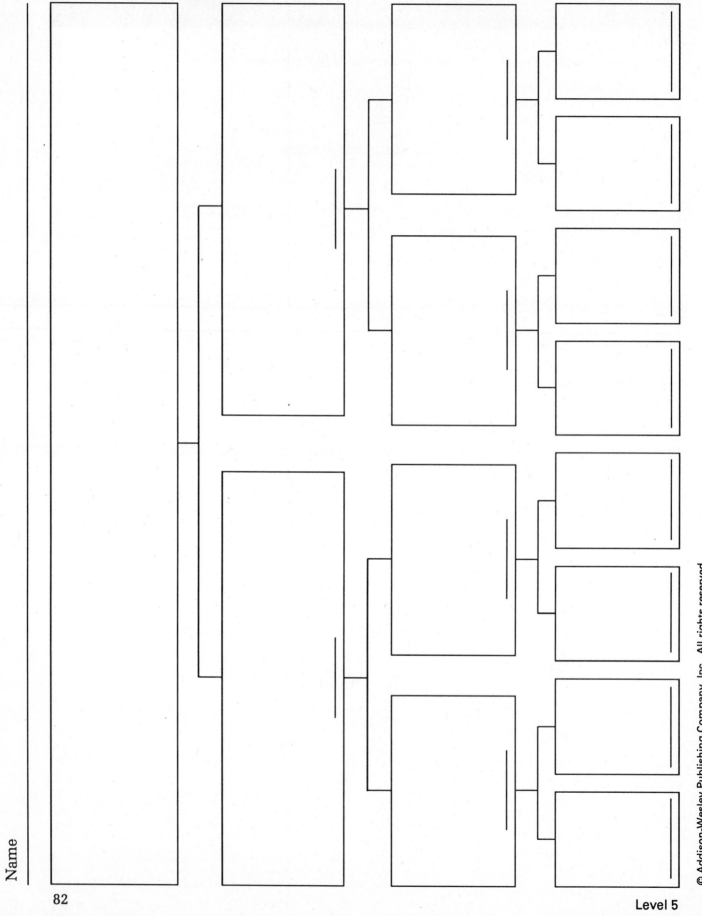

INFERRING

1. Slide the straw marked in centimeters into each of the numbered holes in the shoebox lid. Record the distance to the bottom of the box from each of the holes in the graph below by placing a dot to indicate the depth of each hole and then connecting the dots.

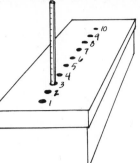

Distance to Bottom of Box

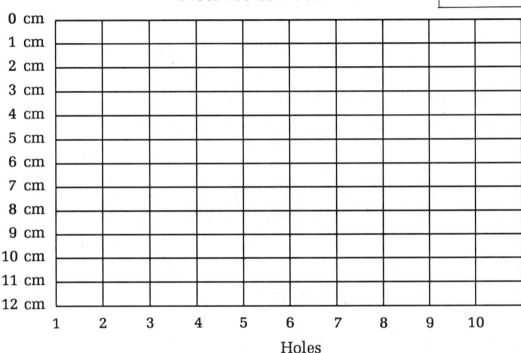

Holes

2. Based on your observations, make a drawing of what you infer the bottom of the box looks like.

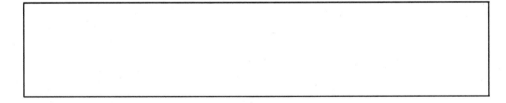

3. Remove the lid and compare your drawing to the bottom of the box. How does your drawing differ from the bottom of the box?

_____

_____

PREDICTING

1. Toss the die 60 times and put a tally mark next to the number on top of the die after each toss. Count the tally marks to determine the number of times the die landed with each numeral on top.

Number on Top of Die	Tally Marks	Total
1		
2		
3		
4		
5		
6		

2. Predict how many times the die would land with each number on top if you tossed it 30 more times.

1 _____   3 _____   5 _____

2 _____   4 _____   6 _____

3. Toss the die 30 more times and record the results.

Number on Top of Die	Tally Marks	Total
1		
2		
3		
4		
5		
6		

4. How close was your prediction to the actual numbers?

_____

5. Why do you think your prediction differed from the actual numbers?

_____

MAKING MODELS

1. The nuts and bolts represent atoms and you will put them together to represent molecules. You will write formulas for each molecule. Use the following symbols:

    Lo (long bolt)   Sh (short bolt)   Wg (wing nut)   Hx (hex nut)

2. Place a hex nut on a long bolt. The formula of this "molecule" is LoHx. If you add another hex nut, the formula is LoHx$_2$.

3. Use the nuts and bolts to make molecules and write the formula for each molecule in the chart below. Record how many nuts and bolts were used in each molecule model.

Molecule Formulas

Long bolts	Short bolts	Wing nuts	Hex nuts	Formula

4. How are your formulas similar to those used by scientists for molecules?

_____

_____

INTERPRETING DATA

1. Look at the graph of information about snakes of the world.

2. Answer the questions about the information in the graph. You may use the calculator.

Snakes of the World

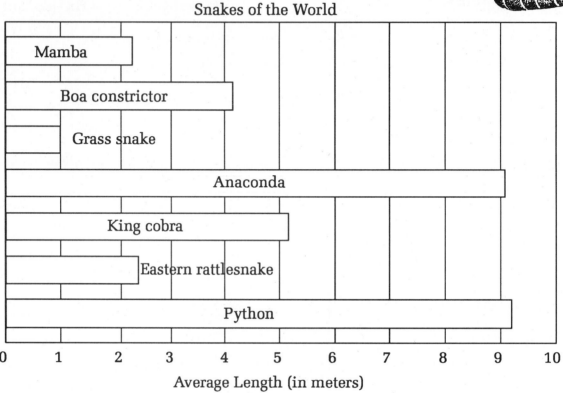

Average Length (in meters)

3. How long is the shortest snake? _____

4. How long is the longest snake? _____

5. What is the difference in length between the longest and shortest snake? _____

6. How much longer is the anaconda than the king cobra? _____

7. How much longer is the python than the boa constrictor? _____

8. How much longer is the king cobra than the mamba? _____

9. List the snakes in order from longest to shortest.

_____

_____

MAKING GRAPHS

1. Slide the rubber tube into the smallest water-filled beaker. When the tube fills with water, pinch one end closed.

2. Pull the pinched end out and down the side of the beaker until it is below the bottom of the beaker.

3. Release the pinched end over the large container.

4. Record the time required to empty the beaker.

5. Repeat the procedure for the other three beakers.

Siphoning Beakers

Beaker	Size of Beaker	Time Required to Empty Beaker
1		
2		
3		
4		

6. Graph the results of this activity. Title the graph, use numerals on each column to indicate the size of each beaker, and use numerals on each row to indicate the time required to empty each beaker. Label the columns and the rows.

Title _____

HYPOTHESIZING

1. Estimate the order of the six objects from longest to shortest drop time when the objects are placed in the cylinder of water. Write the number of each object on the lines below.

   Longest Drop Time ———————————➤ Shortest Drop Time

   ——— ——— ——— ——— ——— ———

2. **Question:** How do the properties of an object (size, shape, volume, density, and weight) affect how fast it will fall through a liquid?

   Your hypothesis (educated guess): _____

   _____

   _____

3. Drop each object into the cylinder of water and record how long it takes the object to reach the bottom.

   Drop Times

Object Number	Drop Time
1	
2	
3	
4	
5	
6	

4. Order the six objects from longest to shortest drop time based on the actual drop times. Write the number of each object on the lines below.

   Longest Drop Time ———————————➤ Shortest Drop Time

   ——— ——— ——— ——— ——— ———

5. Which properties contributed to a fast drop time?

_____

_____

_____

6. State the relationship between properties of an object and drop time.

_____

_____

_____

CONTROLLING VARIABLES

1. Add 1 teaspoon (5 ml) of salt to the 250-ml container of water. Stir until the salt is completely dissolved.

2. Record the length of time required for the salt to dissolve in the chart below.

3. Repeat this procedure using 2 teaspoons, 3 teaspoons, 4 teaspoons, and 5 teaspoons of salt. Important: Always start with fresh water before adding any salt.

Length of Time for Salt to Dissolve

Amount of Salt	Length of Time for Salt to Dissolve
1 teaspoon	
2 teaspoons	
3 teaspoons	
4 teaspoons	
5 teaspoons	

4. Which variable did you change?

_____

5. Which variable responded to the change (what did you time)?

_____

6. Which variables were kept constant?

_____

_____

7. What did you find out about how the amount of salt affects the length of time it takes the salt to dissolve?

_____

_____

_____

DEFINING OPERATIONALLY

1. Look at the diagram. Use the
   materials to construct a model
   of an insect.

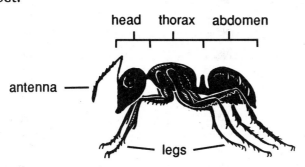

2. Describe your insect model to give your operational
   definition of an insect.

   _____

   _____

   _____

   _____

3. Look up *insect* in your science book or the dictionary and
   write the definition given in the book.

   _____

   _____

   _____

   _____

4. How is your definition of an insect different from the
   definition given in the book?

   _____

   _____

   _____

INVESTIGATING

1. **Problem:** Which of these magnets is the strongest? In this activity you will design and conduct an investigation to help you find out.

2. Describe what you will do to find out which magnet is the strongest.

   _____

   _____

   _____

   _____

   _____

3. Construct a chart to show your results.

Type of Magnet	Number of Paper Clips Picked Up			
	Trial 1	Trial 2	Trial 3	Average

4. Graph the results listed in your chart.

Paper Clips Picked up by Magnets

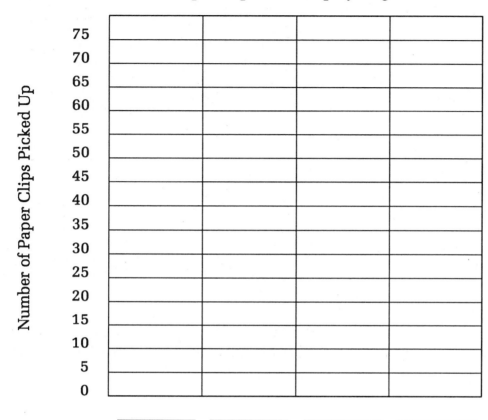

Type of Magnet

5. **Conclusion:** Which of these magnets is the strongest?

_____

6. What did you learn from this investigation?

_____

_____

_____

_____

OBSERVING

Materials
Observing assessment sheet
corn starch and water mixture in a pie tin (mix
   16 oz. of cornstarch with 1⅔ cups of water)
pint-sized container

Procedure
Have the student observe the corn starch and
water mixture using the senses of sight,
smell, and touch. Ask the student to describe
the mixture's color, texture, shape, and odor.
Tell the student to try to poke a finger into
the mixture quickly, and then slowly. Ask the
student to pound on the mixture with a fist.
Have the student pick up some of the
mixture and try to roll it into a ball. Ask the
student to pour the mixture into the
container. Have the student record all
observations on the assessment sheet.

COMMUNICATING

Materials
Communicating assessment sheet
piece of popcorn
unpopped kernel of corn

Procedure
Tell the student to describe the properties of
the piece of popcorn and the kernel of corn.
Then have the student describe the
differences between the two pieces of corn.
Finally, have the student draw pictures to
show how to make popcorn.

ESTIMATING

Materials
Estimating assessment sheet
a science book

Procedure
Explain that the student will estimate the

number of words in the book. Have the
student open to any page and count the
number of words in any one sentence and the
number of sentences in the paragraph. Then
have the student multiply these two numbers,
and then multiply the result by the number of
paragraphs on the page.
   Tell the student to randomly open the
book to another page, count the number of
words in one paragraph and the number of
paragraphs on the page, and to record the
information on the sheet. Ask the student to
multiply the result by the number of
paragraphs on the page to get the number of
words per page. Then have the student
multiply this number by the number of pages
in the book.
   Repeat this procedure with two
consecutive paragraphs on a randomly
selected page. Have the student divide the
number of words in the two paragraphs by
two to get an average number of words per
paragraph. Finally, allow each student to
devise and describe another technique for
sampling and estimating the number of
words in the book.

MEASURING

Materials
Measuring assessment sheet
ten jar or can lids of different sizes numbered
   1 through 10 with a permanent pen (such
   as a Sharpie™)
metric tape measure or meter stick
string
calculator

Procedure
Demonstrate how to measure the circumference of a lid to the nearest millimeter by carefully surrounding it with a length of string,
then placing the taut string along the metric
tape measure or meter stick. Have the student
measure and record the circumference of each
lid in the table. Ask the student to measure

and record the diameter of each lid by measuring across the lids with the tape measure or meter stick.Then have the student divide the circumference by the diameter for each lid and record the results. Explain that this is the value of the constant known as *pi* ($\pi = 3.14$). Ask the student to state the relationship between the circumference and diameter of any circle (the ratio of the circumference of a circle to its diameter is always 3.14, or $C/D = 3.14$).

COLLECTING DATA

Materials
Collecting Data assessment sheet
tennis ball
meter stick taped to the wall (the bottom of
    the stick even with the top of the table)

Procedure
Ask the student to drop the tennis ball onto the table from a height of 100 centimeters and record how high the ball bounces. Have the student repeat the procedure of dropping the ball and recording the distance it bounces from the following heights: 80 cm, 60 cm, 40 cm, and 20 cm. Ask the student to graph the data collected. Then have the student answer the questions on the assessment sheet.

CLASSIFYING

Materials
Classifying assessment sheet
8 different beans (a bean soup mix with at
    least 8 different types of beans can be used)
colored markers or pencils

Procedure
Have the student place the eight beans in the box at the top of the assessment sheet. Ask the student to trace around the beans and color them. Then have the student think of a way to divide the beans into two groups (such as color, thickness, length, shape, or texture).

Ask the student to sort the beans into two groups into the two boxes below the box at the top and to list in the boxes the property that was used to sort the beans. Have the student trace around the beans and color them.

Ask the student to sort the beans in each box into two more groups. Have the student trace and color the beans and list the property that was used this time to sort the beans.

Finally, have the student separate each of these groups so each bean is in a box by itself. Have the student trace and color the beans and list the property used to sort the beans.

INFERRING

Materials
Inferring assessment sheet
string
5 cardboard shapes (circle, triangle, rectangle,
    ellipse, and square), each with two small
    holes at the opposite sides and a 50-cm
    loop of string through each pair of holes

Procedure
Explain that three-dimensional shapes can be generated by rotating two-dimensional shapes. Have the student observe each of the cardboard shapes and infer what three-dimensional shape would be generated by rotating it. Tell the student to record the names of the three-dimensional shapes or to describe them.

Have the student hold the ends of both string loops in one hand, wind the shape with the other hand, and then take the end of one of the string loops in each hand and gently pull in opposite directions. Have the student observe the rotating shape to check his or her inferences. Ask the student to record observations and inferences. *(Note: circle → sphere, triangle → cone, rectangle → cylinder, ellipse → ellipsoid, square → double cone or cylinder.)*

PREDICTING

Materials
Predicting assessment sheet
penny
nickel

dime
quarter
eye dropper
cup of water

Procedure

Ask the student to use the eyedropper to put as many drops of water as possible on the penny until a drop spills over. Have the student record the number of drops. Then have the student predict how many drops of water the other coins will hold before a drop spills over. Ask each student to test the predictions and record the results.

MAKING MODELS

Materials

Making Models assessment sheet
round balloon
black felt-tip marker

Procedure

Explain that the student will make a model to show how air particles move as air is heated and cooled. Have the student use the marker to draw dots on the balloon. Ask the student to inflate the balloon and observe what happens to the dots. Then have the student let the air out of the balloon and observe the dots. Have the student compare the movement of the dots on the inflating and deflating balloon to the movement of particles of air when heated and cooled.

INTERPRETING DATA

Materials

Interpreting Data assessment sheet
calculator

Procedure

Explain that the calculator can be used to answer the questions about paper towels. Have the student complete the table of information about paper towels and answer the questions on the assessment sheet.

MAKING GRAPHS

Materials

Making Graphs assessment sheet
meter stick
eye dropper
1 sheet of red, green, or blue construction
    paper
small container filled with water

Procedure

Have students place the meter stick with the 0-cm end on the construction paper, and drop one drop of water from 10 cm to 100 cm, in 10-cm increments, onto the paper. Have them place the eye dropper next to the meter stick so the **tip** is even with each of these centimeter marks. (If the students drop the water too close to the meter stick, the drop will hit the end of the meter stick.) Have them draw around the wet spot, label the spot with the distance from which the drop fell, and move the meter stick to another area of the paper for the next drop. Have them record measurements in the chart and fill in the graph.

HYPOTHESIZING

Materials

Hypothesizing assessment sheet
tennis ball can with four holes punched up
    the side (the first hole should be at least
    4 cm from the top of the can)
water
plastic dishpan
tape for covering the holes in the can

Procedure

Explain that hypotheses are educated guesses about the answer to a question. Tell each student to give a hypothesis (educated guess) to answer the following question: What is the relationship between the height of the hole in the can and the stream of water coming from it when the can is filled with water?

Ask the student to draw lines on the diagram from the holes in the can to indicate how far out the streams of water will travel. Then have each student test the hypothesis by filling the can with water, quickly removing the tape from the holes, holding the can over the dish pan, and observing the stream of water from each hole. Have the student draw lines on the diagram to represent the actual stream of water from each hole. Then have the student compare the hypothesis to the results and tell whether or not the hypothesis was correct.

CONTROLLING VARIABLES

Materials
Controlling Variables assessment sheet
rubber band
metric tape measure
jumbo paper clip
8 washers
pencil
tape

Procedure
Demonstrate how to tape the pencil to the table so that half of the pencil is hanging over the edge. Show the student how to hang the rubber band on the pencil and attach the paper clip to the bottom. Ask the student to use the metric tape measure to measure the length of the rubber band and record the measurement in the table. Then have the student place one washer on the paper clip and measure the length of the rubber band again. Tell the student to repeat adding a washer, measuring the rubber band, and recording the measurement until all eight washers are hanging from the paper clip. Then have the student answer the questions on the assessment sheet.

DEFINING OPERATIONALLY

Materials
Defining Operationally assessment sheet
peanut in the shell
string bean
science book or dictionary

Procedure
Have the student open the peanut shell and carefully separate each peanut into halves. Then ask the student to draw a cross section of the peanuts in the shell. Have the student repeat this procedure with the string bean. Ask the student how the two cross sections are alike. Explain that the peanut and string bean are both legumes. Have the student write a definition of a legume based on this activity. Then have the student look up the definition of a legume in a science book or dictionary and compare the definition in the book with their own definition.

INVESTIGATING

Materials
Investigating assessment sheet
4 rubber bands of equal length but different widths
pencil with an eraser
tape
jumbo paper clip
500-gram weight (or washers equal to 500 grams)
metric ruler

Procedure
Tape a pencil to the table with the eraser extending over the edge of the table. It will be used as an anchor on which to hang the rubber band. Explain that the student will design an investigation to solve a problem. The problem is to determine which rubber band will stretch the most when weight is added to a jumbo paper clip attached to the bottom of the rubber band. Explain that there are many ways to solve the problem, but that it must be a "fair" test for all the rubber bands

OBSERVING

1. Use the senses of sight, smell, and touch to describe the mixture.

   Color: _____

   Texture: _____

   Shape: _____

   Odor: _____

2. Poke your finger into the mixture quickly. Describe what happens.

   _____

   _____

3. Poke your finger into the mixture slowly. Describe what happens.

   _____

   _____

4. Tap the mixture in the pie tin with you fist. Describe what happens.

   _____

   _____

5. Pick up some of the mixture and roll it into a ball. Describe what happens.

   _____

   _____

6. Pour the mixture into the container. Describe what happens.

   _____

   _____

Level 6

COMMUNICATING

1. Describe the properties of the piece of popcorn (such as color, size, and shape).

   _____

   _____

2. Describe the properties of the kernel of corn.

   _____

   _____

3. Describe the differences between the piece of popcorn and the kernel of corn.

   _____

   _____

4. Draw pictures in the boxes to show someone how to make popcorn.

1	2	3
4	5	6

5. Study your pictures. Did you forget any steps? Write them below.

   _____

ESTIMATING

1. Open the science book to any page. Count the number of words in one sentence. Count the number of sentences in the paragraph. This is called a *sample* from the book.

   ____ words per sentence × ____ sentences per paragraph= ____words per paragraph

2. Multiply the number of words per paragraph by the number of paragraphs on the page. Use the area to the right to do your calculations.

   Number of words per paragraph × number of paragraphs on the page = _____

3. Open the science book to another page. Count the number of words in one paragraph. Count the number of paragraphs on the page. This is a sample of one paragraph.

   _____ words in 1 paragraph × _____ paragraphs per page = _____words per page

4. Multiply the result by the number of pages in the book.

   Number of words per page × number of pages in the book = _____

5. Open the science book to another page. Count the number of words in two consecutive paragraphs. Count the number of paragraphs on the page. This is a sample of two paragraphs.

   _____ words in 2 paragraphs ÷ 2 = _____ words per paragraph ×
   _____ paragraphs per page = _____ words per page

6. Multiply the result by the number of pages in the book.

   Number of words per page × number of pages in the book = _____

7. Devise your own method of sampling the paragraphs to estimate the number of words in the book. Describe your technique.

   _____

   _____

   _____

8. Your estimate of the number of words: _____ words

MEASURING

1. Carefully surround Lid 1 with a length of string. Then hold the string taut along the metric tape measure or meter stick and determine the circumference to the nearest millimeter. Record the measurement in the chart below. Repeat with the other lids.

2. Measure the diameter to the nearest millimeter of each lid by placing the metric tape measure or meter stick across each lid. Record the measurements in the chart below.

Lid Number	Circumference in mm	Diameter in mm	Circumference ÷ Diameter
1			
2			
3			
4			
5			
6			
7			
8			
9			
10			

3. For each lid, use the calculator to divide the circumference by the diameter. Record the result in the chart above.

4. Look at the results in the last column. What can be said about the result when the circumference of any circle is divided by its diameter?

_____

_____

5. This is the value of the constant known as pi (π).

6. What is the relationship between the circumference and diameter of any circle?

_____

_____

COLLECTING DATA

1. Drop the tennis ball onto the table from a height of 100 centimeters and record in the chart below how high the ball bounces.

2. Drop the ball and record the distance it bounces from each of the following heights: 80 cm, 60 cm, 40 cm, and 20 cm.

Height from Which Ball Was Dropped	Height to Which Ball Bounces
100 cm	
80 cm	
60 cm	
40 cm	
20 cm	

3. Construct a graph of the data collected.

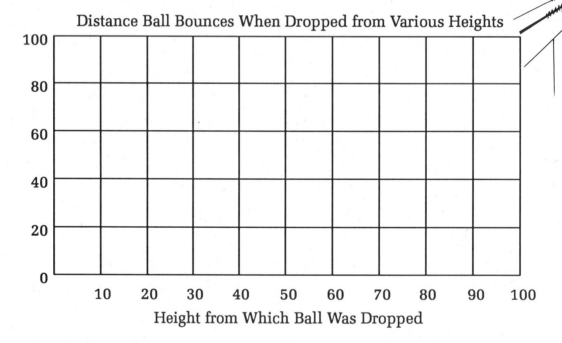

Distance Ball Bounces When Dropped from Various Heights

Height from Which Ball Was Dropped

4. What is the relationship between the height from which the ball is dropped and the distance it bounces?

_____

_____

CLASSIFYING

1. Place the eight beans in the box at the top.

2. Trace around the beans and color them.

3. Divide the beans into two groups in the boxes below the large box.

4. Trace around the beans and color them. In the boxes, write the property you used to sort the beans.

5. Repeat grouping the beans from each box into the two boxes below each box.

6. Trace around the beans and color them. Write the property you used to sort the beans.

7. Place one bean in each of the boxes at the bottom.

8. Trace around each bean and color it. Write the property you used to sort each bean in the box.

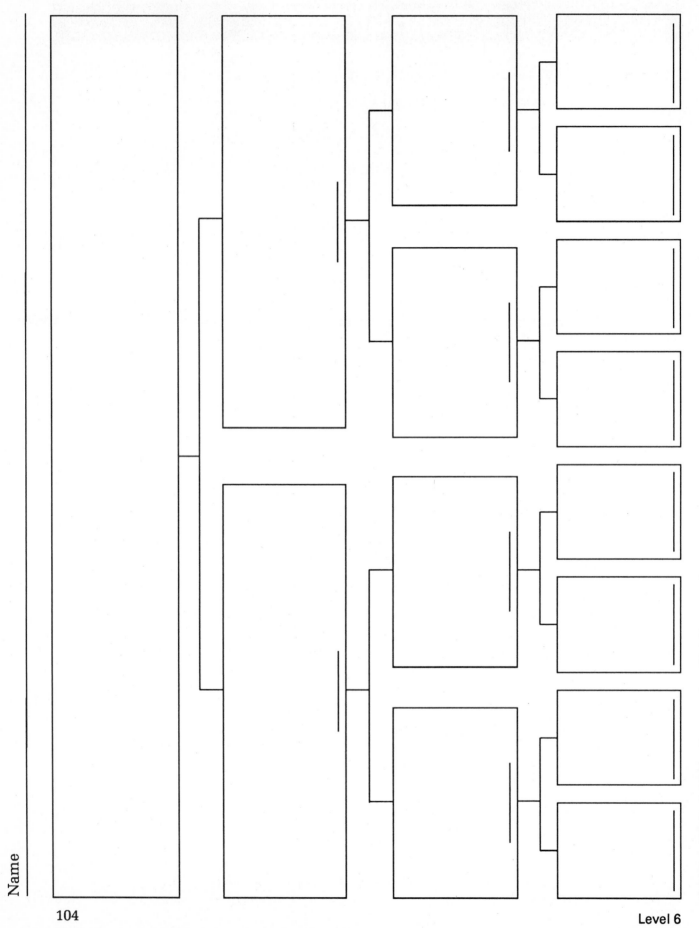

INFERRING

1. Look at each cardboard shape and infer what three-dimensional shape would be generated by rotating it. Write the name for each three-dimensional shape or describe the shape in the chart below.

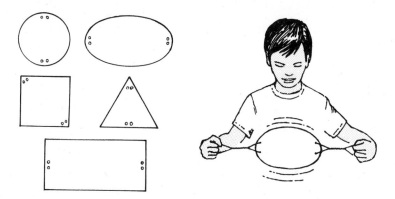

Two-Dimensional Shape	Three-Dimensional Shape Generated by Rotation
circle	
triangle	
rectangle	
ellipse	
square	

2. Hold the string loops in one hand and wind the shape with the other hand. Take the string loops in each hand and gently pull in opposite directions.

3. Observe the rotating shapes. How many of your inferences were correct? _____

4. Write the name of the two-dimensional shapes that did not produce the three-dimensional shapes you inferred and describe or name the three-dimensional shapes actually generated by rotation.

_____

_____

PREDICTING

1. Use the eye dropper to place as many drops as possible on the penny until a drop spills over. Record the number of drops.

   Drops of water a penny will hold: _____ drops

2. Compare the size and shape of the penny with the other coins. Predict how many drops of water each of the other coins will hold.

Coin	Predicted Number of Drops	Actual Number of Drops
Nickel		
Dime		
Quarter		

3. Test your predictions by using the eye dropper to place drops of water on each of the coins until a drop spills over.

4. If your predicted amounts did not match your actual amounts, what could account for the differences?

   _____

   _____

   _____

MAKING MODELS

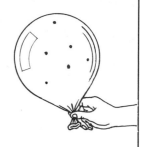

1. In this activity, you will make a model with your balloon to show how air particles move as air is heated and cooled.

2. Draw dots on the balloon with the marker.

3. Blow up the balloon and hold the end closed. Describe what happens to the dots as the balloon inflates.

    _____

    _____

4. Slowly let the air out of the balloon. Describe what happens to the dots as the balloon deflates.

    _____

    _____

5. If this model shows how air particles move as air is heated and cooled, what do the dots represent?

    _____

6. What does the process of blowing up the balloon represent?

    _____

7. What does the process of letting the air out of the balloon represent?

    _____

    _____

    _____

8. Explain how this balloon model acts like the particles in air being heated and cooled.

    _____

    _____

    _____

    _____

1. Look at the following table of information from *Consumer Reports*, September, 1987.

Paper Towels

Paper Towel	Price per roll	Towels per roll	Square Feet per roll	Cost per towel (price ÷ towels)	Cost per Sq. Ft. (price ÷ sq. ft. per roll)
Job Squad	92¢	50	40		
Viva	83¢	90	71		
Bounty	96¢	88	73		
Brawny	77¢	70	73		
ScotTowels	74¢	124	88		
Coronet	71¢	115	79		
Hi-Dri	67¢	100	74		
Zee	76¢	102	72		
Delta	59¢	110	75		
Gala	76¢	110	77		

2. Calculate the cost per towel of each of the brands. (Divide the price by the number of towels per roll.)

3. Calculate the cost per square foot of each brand of paper towels. (Divide the price by the number of square feet per roll.)

4. Which brand costs the least per towel? _____

5. Which brand costs the most per towel? _____

6. Which brand costs the least per square foot? _____

7. Which brand costs the most per square foot? _____

8. Which brand is the "best buy"? _____

   Why ? _____

   _____

MAKING GRAPHS

1. Fill the eye dropper with water.

2. Place the meter stick with the 0-cm end on the construction paper.

3. Release one drop of water from 10 cm, 20 cm, 30 cm, 40 cm, 50 cm, 60 cm, 70 cm, 80 cm, 90 cm, and 100 cm onto the paper. Be sure the tip of the eye dropper is even with each of these centimeter marks. Do not hold the dropper too close to the meter stick or the drop will hit the end of the meter stick.

4. Draw around the wet spot and label the spot with the distance from which the drop fell. Do not draw around splash lines.

5. Move the meter stick after each drop so the next drop lands on a different area of the paper.

6. Measure the diameter of each drop in millimeters at the widest point and record the measurement in the chart on the following page.

7. Graph your results in the graph on the following page. Use numerals along the bottom to indicate the distance and numerals along the side to indicate diameter.

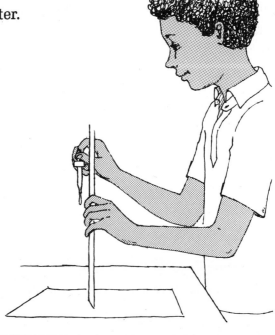

Distance Dropped	Diameter of spot at widest distance (in mm)
10 cm	
20 cm	
30 cm	
40 cm	
50 cm	
60 cm	
70 cm	
80 cm	
90 cm	
100 cm	

Title _____

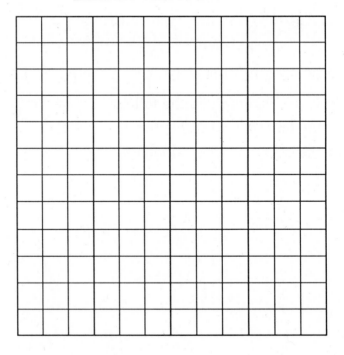

_____

8. State the relationship between the height from which you dropped the water and the diameter of the spot created. _____

_____

HYPOTHESIZING

1. Hypotheses are educated guesses about the answer to a question. Give your hypothesis to answer the following question.

2. **Question:** What is the relationship between the height of the hole in the can and the stream of water coming from it when the can is filled with water?

   Your hypothesis: _____

   _____

3. Draw lines on the diagram to show how far the stream of water will travel from each hole.

4. Cover each hole with tape. Then test your hypothesis by filling the can with water and quickly removing the tape from each of the holes. Hold the can over the dishpan and observe the stream of water from each hole.

5. Draw lines on the diagram below to show the actual stream of water from each hole.

6. Was your hypothesis supported by your observations?

   _____

   _____

CONTROLLING VARIABLES

1. Tape the pencil to the table so that half of the pencil is hanging over the edge.

2. Hang the rubber band on the pencil and attach the paper clip to the bottom of the rubber band.

3. Use the metric tape measure to measure the length of the rubber band. Record this measurement in the table below.

4. Place a washer on the paper clip and measure the length of the rubber band again. Record the measurement in the table below.

5. Repeat adding a washer, measuring the rubber band, and recording the measurement until all eight washers are on the paper clip.

The Stretching Rubber Band

Number of Washers	Length of Rubber Band
0 Washers	
1 Washer	
2 Washers	
3 Washers	
4 Washers	
5 Washers	
6 Washers	
7 Washers	
8 Washers	

6. Which variable did you change?

_____

_____

7. Which variable responded to the change (what did you measure)?

_____

_____

8. Which variables were kept constant?

_____

_____

9. What is the relationship between the length of the rubber band and the number of washers added?

_____

_____

_____

_____

DEFINING OPERATIONALLY

1. Carefully open the peanut and separate the shell. Draw a cross section of the peanut in the box below.

2. Carefully open the string bean and separate the pod. Draw a cross section of the string bean in the box below.

3. How are the cross sections of the peanut and the string bean alike?

_____

_____

4. The peanut and the string bean belong to a group of plants called *legumes*. Write your definition of a legume based on the characteristics that the peanut and the string bean have in common.

_____

_____

5. Look up *legume* in your science book or dictionary and write the definition given in the book.

_____

_____

6. How is your definition of a legume different from the book's definition?

_____

_____

INVESTIGATING

1. **Problem:** Which rubber band will stretch the most when
    500 grams of weight are added? Design and conduct an
    investigation to help you find out.

2. Describe what you will do to find out which rubber band
    stretches the most when 500 grams of weight are added.

    _____

    _____

    _____

    _____

    _____

3. Construct a chart to show your results.

Rubber Band Width	Length before Weight	Length after Weight	Difference

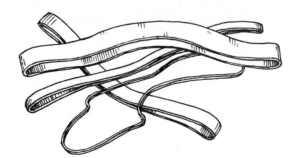

4. Graph the results listed in your chart.

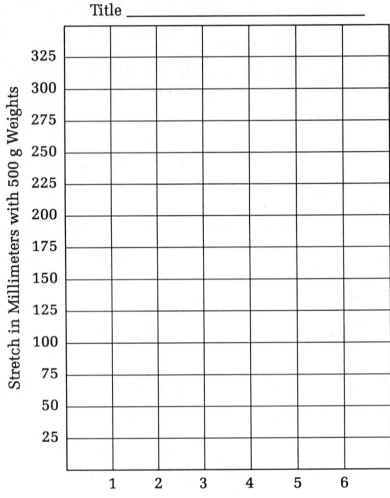

Title _____

Stretch in Millimeters with 500 g Weights

325 · 300 · 275 · 250 · 225 · 200 · 175 · 150 · 125 · 100 · 75 · 50 · 25

1 2 3 4 5 6

Width of Rubber Band in Millimeters

5. **Conclusion:** Which rubber band stretches the most?

_____

_____

_____

6. What did you learn from this investigation?

_____

_____

_____

_____

Student answers will vary. Please do each activity beforehand, as materials and equipment
will affect outcomes. These answers are a guide to indicate trends you can expect in the data.

OBSERVING

1. Put a pair of matching buttons in each box.
2. Trace around the buttons.
3. Color the buttons and draw dots to show the holes.

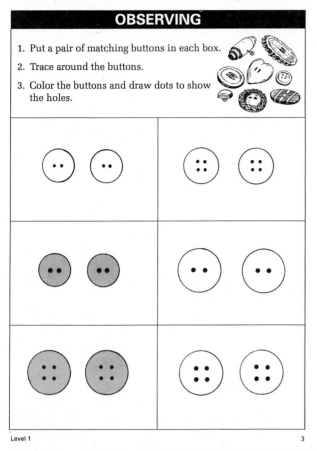

Level 1   3

COMMUNICATING

Draw a picture of an animal that moves in each way.

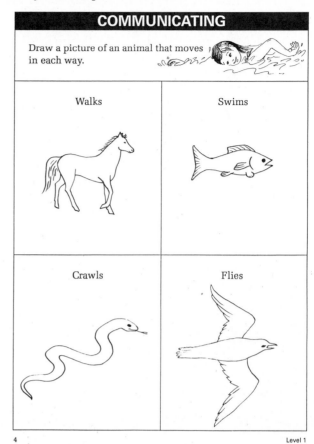

4   Level 1

ESTIMATING

1. Use your finger to estimate how long each line is in centimeters.
2. Write the number in the box.

1 cm
2 cm
3 cm
4 cm
5 cm

10

5

11

4

14

5

Level 1   5

MEASURING

1. Place the strips that are the same length in the same box.
2. Glue down the strips in each box.

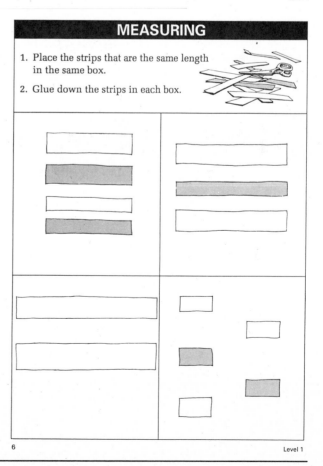

6   Level 1

Student answers will vary. Please do each activity beforehand, as materials and equipment will affect outcomes. These answers are a guide to indicate trends you can expect in the data.

COLLECTING DATA

1. Put the squares that are the same color in the same column.

2. Glue the squares down.

3. Count the squares in each column and write the number in the circle below each column.

④ ⑤ ② ③ ⑥

CLASSIFYING

1. Sort the stones into two groups in the circles below.

2. Trace around the stones and color them.

3. How are the stones in the two groups different?
   Light and dark

4. How are the stones in each group alike?
   Irregular in shape
   Same size

INFERRING

1. Put your hand in the sock.

2. How does the object feel?
   Hard, rough, rounded on the ends,
   smaller than my hand

3. Draw a picture of how you think the object in the sock looks.

PREDICTING

1. Stretch the thinnest rubber band around the box and pluck it.

2. Do the same thing with the thickest rubber band.

3. In the boxes, put the rubber bands in order from the highest to the lowest sound you think they would make. Trace around them and color them.

highest pitch

lowest pitch

Student answers will vary. Please do each activity beforehand, as materials and equipment will affect outcomes. These answers are a guide to indicate trends you can expect in the data.

---

4. Now test all the rubber bands.

5. Tape the rubber bands into the boxes in order from the highest to lowest sound they made.

highest pitch

lowest pitch

6. Are the rubber bands in the same order as your drawings?

Yes ___✓___   No _____

OBSERVING

1. Use your eyes and hands to observe one of the nuts.

2. Describe the nut.

Color _Medium brown with light brown top_

Shape _One end is pointed, one is flat_

Size _Slightly larger than my thumb_

Texture _Feels bumpy_

Special features _Shell has a crack_

3. Draw a picture of your nut in the box.

4. Mix your nut with the other nuts.

5. Find your nut and draw it in the box.

6. Describe the features that helped you find your nut.
The crack in the shell

COMMUNICATING

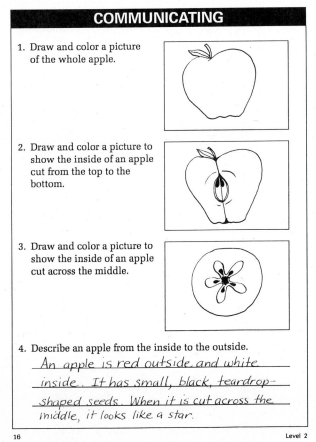

1. Draw and color a picture of the whole apple.

2. Draw and color a picture to show the inside of an apple cut from the top to the bottom.

3. Draw and color a picture to show the inside of an apple cut across the middle.

4. Describe an apple from the inside to the outside.
An apple is red outside and white
inside. It has small, black, teardrop-
shaped seeds. When it is cut across the
middle, it looks like a star.

ESTIMATING

1. Use the square to estimate the number of square centimeters in each of the shapes below.

2. Write your estimate in the circle next to the shape.

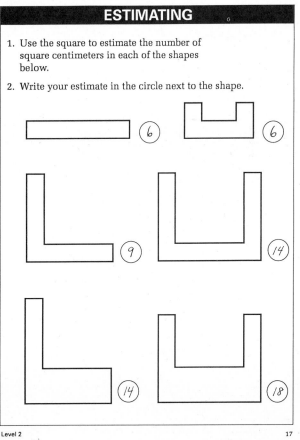

Student answers will vary. Please do each activity beforehand, as materials and equipment will affect outcomes. These answers are a guide to indicate trends you can expect in the data.

MEASURING

1. Estimate the order of the containers from smallest to largest. Write the number of each container on the lines in order.

   Smallest ⟶ Largest
   $\underline{2}$ $\underline{4}$ $\underline{6}$ $\underline{1}$ $\underline{3}$ $\underline{5}$

2. Use the measuring cup to fill each container with water. Write the number of cups used to fill each container.

   Container 1 __4 cups__   Container 4 __2 cups__
   Container 2 __1 cup__   Container 5 __6 cups__
   Container 3 __5 cups__   Container 6 __3 cups__

3. Arrange the containers in order from smallest to largest. Write the number of each container in order.

   Smallest ⟶ Largest
   $\underline{2}$ $\underline{4}$ $\underline{6}$ $\underline{1}$ $\underline{3}$ $\underline{5}$

4. Compare your estimate to the number of cups each container held. Which containers surprised you?

   __My estimate was correct.__

18   Level 2

COLLECTING DATA

1. Sort the buttons into groups by color.

2. Place all the buttons of the same color in a column on the grid.

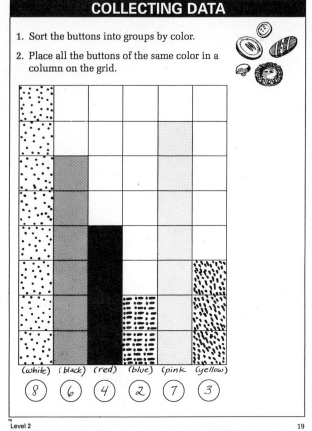

(white) (black) (red) (blue) (pink) (yellow)
⑧ ⑥ ④ ② ⑦ ③

Level 2   19

3. Color the squares covered by a button the same color as the button.

4. How many buttons are in each column? Write the number in the circle below the column.

5. Of which color was the greatest number of buttons?
   __White__

6. Of which color was the least number of buttons?
   __Blue__

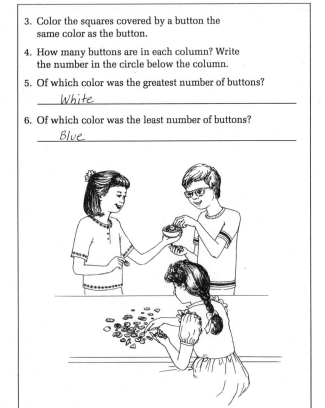

20   Level 1

CLASSIFYING

1. Sort the coins into two groups in the circles below.

(penny)

(quarter)
(dime) (nickel)

__Copper__   __Silver__
Label   Label

2. Trace around each coin.

3. Label each group.

4. How are the coins in each group different?
   __The coins are different sizes and have__
   __different pictures, words, and numbers.__

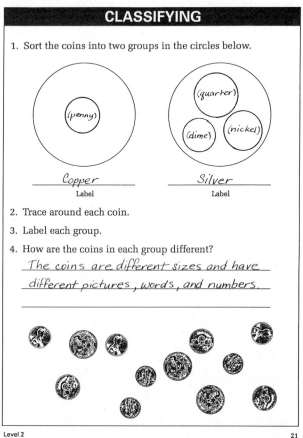

Level 2   21

120   Answers

Student answers will vary. Please do each activity beforehand, as materials and equipment will affect outcomes. These answers are a guide to indicate trends you can expect in the data.

5. Sort the coins into two groups in a different way.

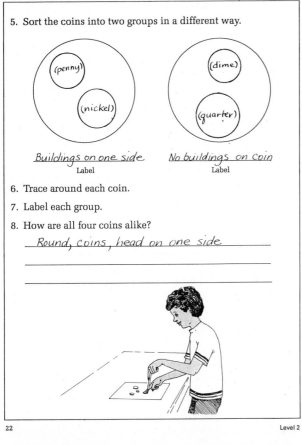

(penny) (nickel)   (dime) (quarter)

Buildings on one side   _No buildings on coin_
　　　　Label　　　　　　　　　　　Label

6. Trace around each coin.

7. Label each group.

8. How are all four coins alike?

Round, coins, head on one side

INFERRING

1. Place the paper shapes on top of the drawings in each row.

2. Look at the pattern of the shapes in each row.

3. In the box at the end of the row, draw the shape that comes next.

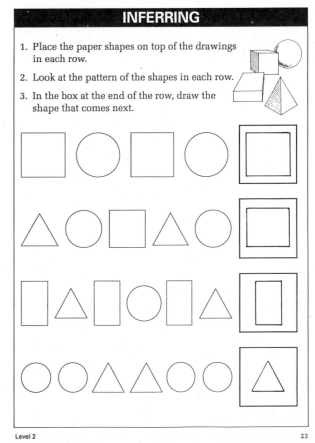

PREDICTING

1. Push one magnet into a pile of 100 paper clips.

2. Count the number of paper clips that stick to the magnet.

3. Record the number in the box. | 5 |

4. Stick three magnets together (use tape if necessary) and push them into a pile of 100 paper clips.

5. Count the number of paper clips that stick to the magnets.

6. Record the number in the box. | 15 |

7. Predict how many paper clips will stick to two magnets. | 10 |

8. Predict how many paper clips will stick to four magnets. | 20 |

9. Record the actual number of paper clips that stick to two magnets. | 10 |

10. Record the actual number of paper clips that stick to four magnets. | 20 |

11. What information did you use to make your predictions?

I observed the number of paper clips
1 magnet and 3 magnets picked up.

MAKING MODELS

1. Cut out the winged seed model on the solid lines.

2. Fold it on the dotted lines.

3. Attach a paper clip to the bottom.

4. Drop the seed model and observe its movement.

5. How does your model show how wind carries seeds?

The model shows how seeds are picked
up by the wind and twirl around.

BOTTOM　　　　　FOLD UP　FOLD DOWN

Answers　　　　　　　　　　　　　　　　　　　　　　**121**

Student answers will vary. Please do each activity beforehand, as materials and equipment will affect outcomes. These answers are a guide to indicate trends you can expect in the data.

OBSERVING

1. What happens when you touch one end of the bar magnet to a paper clip?

   The paper clip sticks to the end of the magnet.

2. Put the magnet on the table. What happens when you touch one end of a paper clip to several places along the sides and at the ends of the magnet?

   The paper clip is attracted most strongly to the center of the end of the magnet, and also along the sides near the ends, but not in the middle of the magnet.

3. Put the magnet on the table. What happens when you slide another magnet toward it so that the N (north) ends of the magnets approach each other?

   When the magnets are about 1cm apart, the magnet slides away and turns sideways.

4. Put the magnet on the table. What happens when you slide another magnet toward it so that the N and S (south) ends of the magnets approach each other?

   When the magnets are about 1cm apart, the magnet on the table moves toward the approaching magnet.

5. Hold the bar magnet in a vertical position and suspend two paper clips from the lower end of the magnet so that the paper clips are side by side with their upper ends against the end of the magnet. What happens to the paper clips?

   The upper ends of the paper clips hanging from the end of the magnet are separated by about 1mm. The lower ends are separated by 1 cm or more.

6. Put two bar magnets on the table with their N and S ends together. Pull the magnets apart and place a paper clip between the ends. Slowly pull the magnets apart until the paper clip is disconnected from one of them. Repeat several times. Does the paper clip disconnect from the both magnets or does it disconnect more often from one magnet?

   The paper clip disconnects from each of the magnets randomly. (However, students may observe that the paper clip disconnects from one magnet every time.)

COMMUNICATING

1. Examine the peanut closely. In the box, trace around the peanut and draw lines to show the shell's pattern.

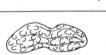

2. Gently break the shell of the peanut and separate the two halves. Draw the inside of the peanut shell in the box.

3. Gently break apart one peanut and separate the two halves. Draw the inside of the peanut in the box below.

4. Look closely at all the parts of the peanut. List the things that are special about this peanut.

   This peanut is smaller at one end than the other and it is darker on one side.

ESTIMATING

1. Use the plastic foam peanuts and containers 1 through 4 to help estimate the number of peanuts in the soda bottle (container 5).

2. Estimate and then count the number of peanuts that each container holds.

Container	Estimate	Actual Number
Container 1	25	25
Container 2	50	50
Container 3	75	75
Container 4	100	100

3. Describe what you did to estimate.

   I compared the size of the peanut to the smallest container. Then I compared the size of the smallest container to the other containers.

4. Estimate how many peanuts are in container 5.

   200 peanuts

5. Describe what you did to estimate.

   I compared the number of peanuts in each container to the peanuts in the soda bottle.

Student answers will vary. Please do each activity beforehand, as materials and equipment will affect outcomes. These answers are a guide to indicate trends you can expect in the data.

COLLECTING DATA

1. Open ten green beans and count the seeds.

2. Record the number of seeds you find in each bean.

Beans	1	2	3	4	5	6	7	8	9	10
Number of Seeds	5	5	6	6	6	5	7	4	5	6

3. Color one square below for each bean that had 3 seeds. Do the same for 4 seeds, 5 seeds, 6 seeds, 7 seeds, 8 seeds, and 9 seeds.

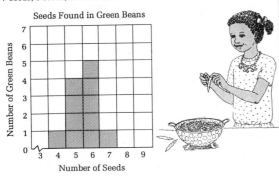

Seeds Found in Green Beans

(y-axis: Number of Green Beans, 0–7; x-axis: Number of Seeds, 3–9)

4. What is the most common number of seeds found in a green bean? ___6___

CLASSIFYING

1. Sort the seeds into two groups in the boxes below.

2. Trace around the seeds and color them. Label each group.

Label _Small_	Label _Large_

3. How are the seeds in each group alike?

  They all have pointed ends.

4. Sort the seeds a different way in the boxes below.

5. Trace around the seeds and color them. Label each group.

Label _Light_	Label _Dark_

6. How are the seeds in each group different?

  Different sizes, different plants.

PREDICTING

1. Pour 20 ml of water into the graduated cylinder.

2. Record the water level in the chart and on the graph.

3. Drop five marbles in the cylinder and record the water level in the chart and on the graph.

4. Add 10 more marbles so you have 15 marbles in the cylinder. Record the water level below.

5. Predict what the water level will be with 10 marbles. ___30___ ml

6. Predict what the water level will be with 20 marbles. ___40___ ml

7. Predict what the water level will be with 25 marbles. ___45___ ml

8. Test each of your predictions with the marbles and the cylinder.

9. Record the actual water level in the chart and on the graph.

Number of Marbles	Water Level in ml.
0	20 ml
5	25 ml
15	35 ml
10	30 ml
20	40 ml
25	45 ml

Changes in Water Level When Marbles Are Added

(y-axis: Water Level in ml., 20–45; x-axis: Number of Marbles, 0–25)

INTERPRETING DATA

1. Use only red, blue, and yellow watercolors to make the color wheel below.

2. You may mix the primary colors (red, blue, and yellow) to make the secondary colors (purple, green, and orange).

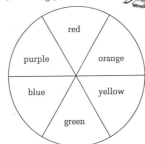

Color wheel: red, purple, orange, blue, yellow, green

3. Which colors did you mix to make orange?   _Red and yellow_

4. Which colors did you mix to make green?   _Yellow and blue_

5. Which colors did you mix to make purple?   _Blue and red_

6. Why do you think the colors are arranged this way on the color wheel?

  The secondary colors are arranged between the two primary colors that are mixed to make each secondary color.

Student answers will vary. Please do each activity beforehand, as materials and equipment will affect outcomes. These answers are a guide to indicate trends you can expect in the data.

MAKING GRAPHS

1. Go to the measuring tape with your partner.

2. Have your partner place the dot on the decimeter mark nearest to your height.

3. When everyone has placed a dot on the measuring tape, complete the chart and the graph below.

Height in Decimeters	10	11	12	13	14	15	16	17
Number of Students	0	2	12	10	4	1	0	0

Title _The Heights of Students_

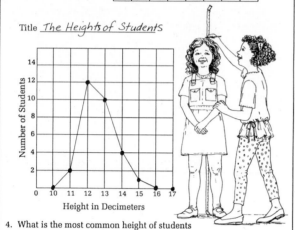

4. What is the most common height of students in your class? _12 dm_

(Note: Graph could also be done as a histogram.)

HYPOTHESIZING

1. **Question:** How does the size of a sponge affect the amount of water it will hold? Your hypothesis (educated guess):

   The larger the sponge, the more water it will hold.

2. Place the 2 cm × 2 cm sponge on the construction paper.
   • Fill the graduated cylinder with water to the 250-ml mark.
   • Pour water 10 ml at a time evenly over the sponge. Each time, lift the sponge. When the paper is wet, stop pouring.
   • Subtract the amount of water left in the cylinder from 250 to find out how much water saturated the sponge.
   • Record this number in the chart below.
   • Refill the graduated cylinder.

3. Repeat with the remaining three sponges.

Sponge Size   250 ml − ____ (water level after saturating sponge) = ____ml

Sponge Size		
2 cm × 2 cm	250 − 230	20 ml
3 cm × 3 cm	250 − 205	45 ml
4 cm × 4 cm	250 − 170	80 ml
5 cm × 5 cm	250 − 125	125 ml

4. Did your investigation support your hypothesis? _yes_

5. Explain. _The larger sponges held more water than the smaller sponges._

CONTROLLING VARIABLES

1. Make a ramp by setting the ruler on top of one of the books or blocks.

2. Roll the marble from the top of the ramp and measure the distance it travels from the end of the ramp.

3. Record the distance in the chart below.

4. Add another book and roll the marble again. Measure the distance it travels from the end of the ramp.

5. Repeat this procedure until the ramp is 6 books high.

Height of Ramp	Distance marble travels from end of ramp in centimeters
1 book	15 cm
2 books	28 cm
3 books	38 cm
4 books	48 cm
5 books	52 cm
6 books	60 cm

6. Which variable did you change?
   The height of the ramp.

7. Which variable responded to the change (what did you measure)?
   The distance the marble travels.

8. Which variables were kept constant?
   Marble, ramp, manner of rolling marble.

DEFINING OPERATIONALLY

1. Carbohydrates give your body quick energy.
   • Carbohydrates include foods that have sugar and starches.
   • Iodine will turn blue-black when placed on something that contains starch.

2. Place a drop of iodine on each of the foods to test whether any of them contain starch.

3. In the chart below, record the color of the iodine on the food.

Food	Color of Iodine	Contains Starch (Yes or No)
potato	Blue-black	yes
bread	Blue-black	yes
pasta	Blue-black	yes
cracker	Blue-black	yes

4. Give your definition of a carbohydrate based on what you did in this activity.
   A carbohydrate turns blue-black when a drop of iodine is placed on it.

Student answers will vary. Please do each activity beforehand, as materials and equipment will affect outcomes. These answers are a guide to indicate trends you can expect in the data.

INVESTIGATING

1. **Problem:** Which of these white powders is baking soda? Design and conduct an investigation to help you find out. *Note: Baking soda will fizz when it comes into contact with an acid such as vinegar.*

2. Describe what you will do to find out which white powder is baking soda.

   I will place 5 drops of vinegar on each powder and observe which powders fizz.

3. Construct a chart to show your results.

Powder	Reaction with Vinegar
1	No fizz
2	No fizz
3	Fizzes
4	No fizz

4. **Conclusion:** Which of these white powders is baking soda?

   Powder 3 is baking soda.

5. What did you learn from this investigation?

   I learned that one of the powders might be baking soda because it fizzed when I added vinegar. I learned that vinegar can be used to test for baking soda.

OBSERVING

1. Use your eyes, ears, hands, and nose to observe the shell.

2. Describe the color of the shell. The indented side is yellowish white. The other side is grayish white.

3. Describe the shape of the shell. The shell is fan-shaped or pie-shaped.

4. Describe the size of the shell. The shell is 3 cm wide and 2½ cm long, size of the end of my thumb.

5. Describe the texture of the shell. The indented side is smooth. The other side has ridges and feels rough.

6. Describe the sound of the shell. The shell sounds solid when I drop it on the table.

7. Describe the odor of the shell. The shell has no odor.

8. Draw and color a picture of the shell in the box below.

COMMUNICATING

Read the ingredients listed on the product label. List the ingredients in order and the amount of each ingredient (if given) in the chart below. (Ingredients on product labels are listed from most to least abundance.)

Name of Product Truffles Potato Chips

Ingredient	Amount of Ingredient (if given)
Potatoes	
Vegetable oil (contains one or more of the following: Sunflower oil, Canola oil, partially hydrogenated Sunflower oil, partially hydrogenated canola oil, partially hydrogenated soybean oil, partially hydrogenated Cottonseed oil)	
Salt	

3. List everything you learned about this product from the label.

   Many different kinds of oil may be in this product. After potatoes, oil is the most abundant ingredient.

ESTIMATING

1. Use the grid in the box and/or the containers to estimate the number of raisins in the box of cereal. (Do not count every raisin.) Use the box below to do your calculations.

   23 raisins × 18 containers = 414 raisins

2. Record your estimate of the number of raisins in the box. 414 raisins

3. Describe what you did to estimate the number of raisins in the box.

   I counted the raisins in one container of cereal. Then I counted how many containers were needed to fill the box. I multiplied the number of raisins times the number of containers.

Answers   125

Student answers will vary. Please do each activity beforehand, as materials and equipment will affect outcomes. These answers are a guide to indicate trends you can expect in the data.

MEASURING

1. Estimate the length of each of your body parts by putting them in order from shortest to longest: the length of the thumb, hand, foot, arm, and leg; the distance around the knee, head, neck, wrist, and ankle.

Body Part	Estimated Order 1=shortest 10=longest	Measurement	Actual Order 1=shortest 10=longest
Thumb	1	5 cm	1
Hand	3	18 cm	3
Foot	4	24 cm	4
Arm	9	53 cm	8
Leg	10	70 cm	10
Knee	8	38 cm	7
Head	5	55 cm	9
Neck	7	32 cm	6
Wrist	2	17 cm	2
Ankle	6	26 cm	5

2. Use the metric tape measure to measure your body parts and write the actual measurements in centimeters.

3. Use the actual measurements to order your body parts from shortest to longest, using 1 for the shortest and 10 for the longest.

4. Compare your estimates with your measurements. How close was your estimated order to the actual order?

5 were incorrect.

5. What surprised you?

My head is much bigger around than I had predicted.

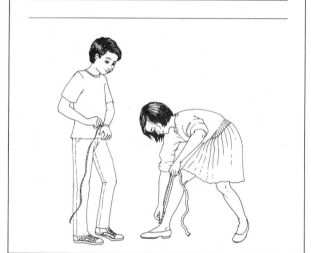

COLLECTING DATA

1. Reach into the sock and remove one paper clip.

2. List the color of the paper clip and put a tally mark in the chart.

3. Remove another paper clip. If the color is different from the first color, list the color in the chart and make a tally mark next to it. If the color is the same as the first color, put another tally mark next to the first color.

4. Continue taking paper clips out of the sock and recording their colors in the chart.

Paper Clips

Color	Tally Marks	Total
Blue	ЖТ ЖТ ЖТ	15
Red	ЖТ ЖТ II	12
Green	ЖТ ЖТ	10
Yellow	ЖТ III	8
Orange	ЖТ	5

5. Fill in the graph on the next page. Color one box for each paper clip. The box should be the same color as the paper clip. Start at the bottom of the graph and use a different color for the boxes in each column. Columns should show how many paper clips you have of each color.

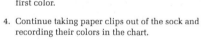

	15				
14				
13				
12				
11				

| Blue | Red | Green | Yellow | Orange |
| color | color | color | color | color |

6. Which color were the greatest number of paper clips? _Blue_

7. Which color were the least number of paper clips? _Orange_

Student answers will vary. Please do each activity beforehand, as materials and equipment will affect outcomes. These answers are a guide to indicate trends you can expect in the data.

CLASSIFYING

1. Sort the screws and bolts into two groups in the circles below.

2. Trace around the screws and bolts and color them.

Label _Round tops_   Label _Hexagonal tops_

3. How are the items in each group alike?

They are all the same color and used to fasten things together.

4. Sort the screws and bolts a different way into two groups in the circles below.

5. Trace around the screws and bolts and color them.

Label _Pointed ends (screws)_ Label _Flat ends (bolts)_

6. How are the items in each group different?

The screws are different sizes, but they all have pointed ends. The bolts have different tops, but they all have flat ends.

INFERRING

1. Look at the advertisement. List an observation and an inference that could be made about the advertisement in the chart below. An example is given for you.

Purr-fect
FLEA POWDER
For Komfy Kitties

Observation	Inference
The woman is petting the cat.	The cat is purring.
The girl is wearing a red shirt.	Red is the girl's favorite color.

2. What do you think the advertisers want you to believe will happen if you use their product?

If you use this product, you will be happy.

PREDICTING

1. Flip the penny 40 times and record in the chart below whether it lands on heads or tails.

Trial No.	1	2	3	4	5	6	7	8	9	10
H or T	H	H	T	H	T	H	H	T	H	T

Trial No.	11	12	13	14	15	16	17	18	19	20
H or T	H	T	H	H	T	T	H	T	T	H

Trial No.	21	22	23	24	25	26	27	28	29	30
H or T	H	T	H	H	T	T	H	T	T	H

Trial No.	31	32	33	34	35	36	37	38	39	40
H or T	T	T	H	T	T	H	T	H	T	H

2. How many times did the penny land on heads? _20_

3. How many times did the penny land on tails? _20_

4. Predict how many times the penny would land on heads and how many times on tails if you flipped it 10 more times.

heads _5_
tails _5_

Answers   127

Student answers will vary. Please do each activity beforehand, as materials and equipment will affect outcomes. These answers are a guide to indicate trends you can expect in the data.

5. Flip the penny 10 more times and record the results in the chart below.

Trial No.	1	2	3	4	5	6	7	8	9	10
H or T	H	T	H	H	T	H	H	H	T	T

6. How many times did the penny land on heads? __6__

7. How many times did the penny land on tails? __4__

8. Explain why your prediction might not match the actual number of heads and tails.

   Because chance is a factor.

MAKING MODELS

1. Outline the teeth in black. Color the gums orange.

2. Cut out the shape on the solid lines. Fold along the dotted lines. Follow the directions for overlapping and gluing the model.

3. How is this model the same as real teeth?

   The teeth are the same in number, size, and position.

4. How is this model different from real teeth?

   The model is made of paper, not enamel.

INTERPRETING DATA

1. Read the table below and answer the questions about the information.

Active Volcanoes of North America

Name (year of latest activity)	Location	Height (in meters)
Colima (1986)	Mexico	4,268
Redoubt (1966)	Alaska	3,108
Iliamna (1978)	Alaska	3,076
Mount St. Helens (1986)	Washington	2,950
Shishaldin (1981)	Aleutian Islands	2,861
Veniaminof (1884)	Alaska	2,507
Pavlof (1984)	Aleutian Islands	2,504
El Chichon (1983)	Mexico	2,225
Makushin (1980)	Aleutian Islands	2,036
Trident (1963)	Alaska	1,832
Great Sitkan (1974)	Aleutian Islands	1,740
Akutan (1980)	Aleutian Islands	1,303
Kiska (1969)	Aleutian Islands	1,303
Sequam (1977)	Alaska	1,054

2. How high is the highest active volcano? __4,268 meters__

3. How high is the lowest active volcano? __1,054 meters__

4. What is the difference in height between the highest and lowest volcano? __3214 meters__

5. What is the most recent date of volcanic activity? __1986__

6. What is the least recent date of volcanic activity? __1884__

7. How many years passed between the most recent activity and the least recent activity? __102 years__

MAKING GRAPHS

1. Work with a partner. One person will hold the centimeter ruler at the 33-cm end. The other person will hold a thumb and index finger at the zero end of the ruler without actually touching it.

2. The person holding the ruler will drop it and the other person will try to catch it as close to the 0-cm mark as possible. Record the cm mark at which the ruler is caught.

3. Repeat for a total of 10 trials.

Response Time

Trial Number	Place (cm) Where Fingers Caught Falling Ruler
1	15 cm
2	14 cm
3	14 cm
4	13 cm
5	13 cm
6	12 cm
7	12 cm
8	11 cm
9	10 cm
10	10 cm

Student answers will vary. Please do each activity beforehand, as materials and equipment will affect outcomes. These answers are a guide to indicate trends you can expect in the data.

4. Graph the results of this activity. Remember to title your graph, use numerals on each column to indicate the trial number, and use numerals on each row to indicate the distance from 0 that the ruler was caught.

Title   My Responses

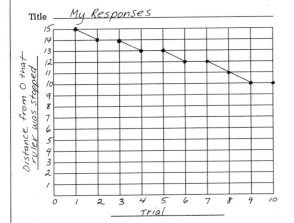

Y-axis: Distance from 0 that ruler was stopped

X-axis: Trial

5. Which trial had the shortest reaction time? 10 and 9

6. Did reaction time improve with practice? Yes

HYPOTHESIZING

1. Cut one end of one of the straws to form a point and blow into this end of the straw to produce a sound. Observe the pitch of the sound produced (high or low).

2. **Question:** How does the length of the straw affect the pitch of the sound produced?

   Your hypothesis (educated guess): The longer the straw, the lower the pitch of the sound produced.

3. Trim the five remaining straws to different lengths. Then cut one end of each straw, blow into this end, and observe the pitch of the sound produced.

4. Arrange your six straws in order from the highest to the lowest pitch and tape the straws in the box below.

Highest

Lowest

5. Did your investigation prove your hypothesis is correct? yes

CONTROLLING VARIABLES

1. Tape the pencil to the table so that it hangs over the edge. Hang the longest pendulum from the pencil. Hold the pendulum even with the top of the table and release it.

2. Count how many times it swings back and forth in 15 seconds and record the number of swings in the chart below. Use the metric tape measure to measure the length of the pendulum. Repeat this procedure with the other five pendulums.

Length of Pendulum in cm	Number of Swings Back and Forth in 15 Seconds
10 cm	20
20 cm	16
30 cm	14
40 cm	11
50 cm	10
60 cm	9

3. Which variable did you change? Length of the pendulum

4. Which variable responded to the change (what did you count)?
   The number of swings in 15 seconds.

5. Which variables were kept constant? Weight, angle of release, anchor point.

6. How does the length of the pendulum affect the number of times it swings in 15 seconds? The longer the length of the pendulum, the fewer the number of swings in 15 seconds.

DEFINING OPERATIONALLY

1. Look at the diagram of the complete circuit. Set up the bulb, dry cell, and wire to make a complete circuit so the bulb lights.

2. Give your definition of a complete circuit based on what you did.
   A circuit is a bulb, dry cell, and wire connected so the bulb lights.

3. Look up *circuit* in your science book or the dictionary and write the definition given in the book.
   The path formed by a conductor for the flow of electric charges.

4. How is your definition of a circuit different from the definition given in the book?
   My definition tells what happens when a circuit is connected.

Student answers will vary. Please do each activity beforehand, as materials and equipment will affect outcomes. These answers are a guide to indicate trends you can expect in the data.

INVESTIGATING

1. **Problem:** Which of these balls bounces the highest? Design and conduct an investigation to find out.

2. Describe what you will do to determine which ball bounces the highest. _I will drop each ball 3 times and record how high each bounces. I will graph the averages to determine which ball bounces the highest._

3. Construct a chart to show your results.

Type of ball	Trial 1	Trial 2	Trial 3	Average
Plastic foam	30 cm	31 cm	32 cm	31 cm
Solid rubber	71 cm	70 cm	72 cm	71 cm
Hollow rubber	63 cm	65 cm	61 cm	63 cm
Plastic	55 cm	54 cm	50 cm	53 cm

4. Graph the results listed in your chart.

Title _Bouncing Balls_

Height Ball Bounces in cm.

Type of Ball

5. **Conclusion:** Which of these balls bounces the highest? _The solid rubber ball._

6. What did you learn from this investigation? _I learned that the solid rubber ball bounced highest. I learned that it is easy to tell which bounced the highest by looking at the graph._

70

Level 4

Level 4

71

OBSERVING

1. Observe the cube using the sense of sight. Describe the cube.
   Color: _White, sparkles_

   Shape: _Cube shaped_

2. Use the metric ruler to make observations about size of the cube.
   Length: _1.3 cm_ Width: _1.3 cm_ Height: _1.3 cm_

3. Observe the cube using the sense of touch. Describe the cube.
   Texture: _Feels hard but crumbly, rough texture._

4. Observe the cube using the sense of hearing. Drop the cube on the table.
   Sound: _Makes a sharp sound when dropped._

5. Observe the cube using the sense of smell. Describe the cube.
   Odor: _Has no distinctive odor._

6. Place the cube in the cup of water and stir. Record your observations.
   Disappears in water.

76

Level 5

COMMUNICATING

1. Use the book to find information about the five groups of vertebrates: fish, amphibians, reptiles, birds, and mammals.

2. Complete the table by listing features of each group of vertebrates and drawing one member of each group.

Vertebrates

Group	Features	Example
Fish	Skeleton, cold-blooded, scales, fins, gills, lay eggs	Shark
Amphibians	Skeleton, cold-blooded, moist skin, gills as young, lungs as adults, lay jellylike eggs in water	Frog
Reptiles	Skeleton, cold-blooded, dry skin, scales, lungs, lay leathery eggs on land	Snake
Birds	Skeleton, warm-blooded, hollow bones, wings, lay hard-shelled eggs	Hummingbird
Mammals	Skeleton, warm-blooded, milk glands, hair or fur, teeth	Dog

Level 5

77

Student answers will vary. Please do each activity beforehand, as materials and equipment will affect outcomes. These answers are a guide to indicate trends you can expect in the data.

ESTIMATING

1. Use the grid in the box and/or the containers to estimate the number of items in each jar.

2. Use the boxes below to do your calculations.

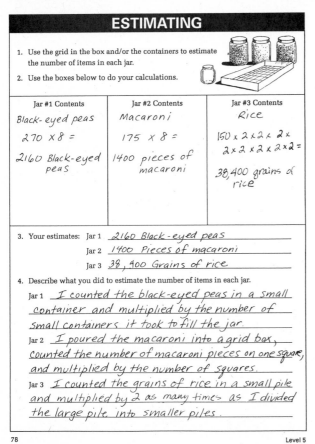

Jar #1 Contents	Jar #2 Contents	Jar #3 Contents
Black-eyed peas	Macaroni	Rice
270 × 8 =	175 × 8 =	150 × 2 × 2 × 2 × 2 × 2 × 2 × 2 × 2 =
2160 Black-eyed peas	1400 pieces of macaroni	38,400 grains of rice

3. Your estimates: Jar 1 _2160 Black-eyed peas_
    Jar 2 _1400 Pieces of macaroni_
    Jar 3 _38,400 Grains of rice_

4. Describe what you did to estimate the number of items in each jar.

    Jar 1 _I counted the black-eyed peas in a small container and multiplied by the number of small containers it took to fill the jar._

    Jar 2 _I poured the macaroni into a grid box, counted the number of macaroni pieces on one square, and multiplied by the number of squares._

    Jar 3 _I counted the grains of rice in a small pile and multiplied by 2 as many times as I divided the large pile into smaller piles._

78   Level 5

MEASURING

1. Estimate the volume of each object by putting the objects in order from smallest volume to greatest volume. List the number on each object.

Smallest ——————————————————————→ Greatest

1	3	6	9	2	4	7	8	5	10

2. Use the graduated cylinder to determine the volume of each object. Fill the cylinder halfway with water. Record the water level, before and after adding each object, in the chart below. The volume of the object is equal to one cubic centimeter (1 cm³) for every milliliter (ml) displaced.

Actual Volume of Objects

Object Number	Water level with object – Beginning water level		Volume = __ ml = __cm³	
1	22 ml -	20 ml	2 ml	2 cm³
2	33 ml -	20 ml	13 ml	13 cm³
3	25 ml -	20 ml	5 ml	5 cm³
4	35 ml -	20 ml	15 ml	15 cm³
5	45 ml -	20 ml	25 ml	25 cm³
6	27 ml -	20 ml	7 ml	7 cm³
7	38 ml -	20 ml	18 ml	18 cm³
8	40 ml -	20 ml	20 ml	20 cm³
9	30 ml -	20 ml	10 ml	10 cm³
10	50 ml -	20 ml	30 ml	30 cm³

3. Order the objects from smallest to greatest volume.

Smallest ——————————————————————→ Greatest

1	3	6	9	2	4	7	8	5	10

Level 5   79

COLLECTING DATA

1. Without looking in the box, take out one colored square. List the color of the square and put a tally mark in the chart.

2. Take out another square. If the color is different from the first color, list the color in the chart and make a tally mark next to it. If the color is the same, put another tally mark next to the first color.

3. Continue taking squares out of the box and recording the color in the chart until you have removed 100 squares.

Color	Tally Marks	Total
Red	̶H̶T̶ ̶H̶T̶ ̶H̶T̶ ̶H̶T̶ ̶H̶T̶ ̶H̶T̶ ̶H̶T̶ ̶H̶T̶ ̶H̶T̶ ̶H̶T̶	50
Blue	̶H̶T̶ ̶H̶T̶ ̶H̶T̶ ̶H̶T̶	20
Green	̶H̶T̶ ̶H̶T̶ ̶H̶T̶	15
Yellow	̶H̶T̶ ̶H̶T̶	10
Orange	̶H̶T̶	5

4. Fill in the graph below. Color boxes for each colored square, the same color as the square. Start at the bottom and use a different color for the boxes in each column. Each column should show how many squares you have of each color.

50						
40						
30						
20						
10						
0						
	Red color	Blue color	Green color	Yellow color	Orange color	color

5. Of which color were the greatest number of squares? _Red_
    Of which color were the least number of squares? _Orange_

80   Level 5

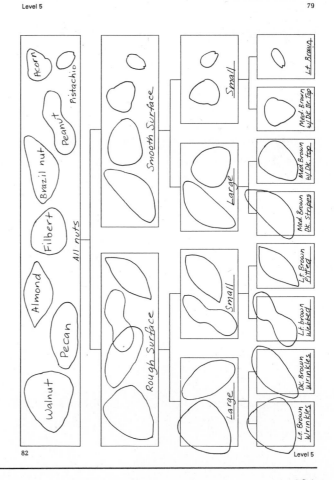

82   Level 5

Answers   131

Student answers will vary. Please do each activity beforehand, as materials and equipment will affect outcomes. These answers are a guide to indicate trends you can expect in the data.

INFERRING

1. Slide the straw marked in centimeters into each of the numbered holes in the shoebox lid. Record the distance to the bottom of the box from each of the holes in the graph below by placing a dot to indicate the depth of each hole and then connecting the dots.

Distance to Bottom of Box

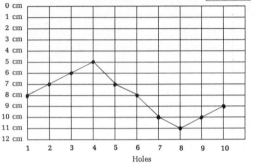

Holes

2. Based on your observations, make a drawing of what you infer the bottom of the box looks like.

3. Remove the lid and compare your drawing to the bottom of the box. How does your drawing differ from the bottom of the box?

The box has more variation in surface than my drawing.

PREDICTING

1. Toss the die 60 times and put a tally mark next to the number on top of the die after each toss. Count the tally marks to determine the number of times the die landed with each numeral on top.

Number on Top of Die	Tally Marks	Total
1	ЖΤ ЖΤ /	11
2	ЖΤ ////	9
3	ЖΤ ////	9
4	ЖΤ ЖΤ //	12
5	ЖΤ ////	9
6	ЖΤ ЖΤ	10

2. Predict how many times the die would land with each number on top if you tossed it 30 more times.

1 _5_   3 _5_   5 _5_

2 _5_   4 _5_   6 _5_

3. Toss the die 30 more times and record the results.

Number on Top of Die	Tally Marks	Total
1	ЖΤ	5
2	ЖΤ //	7
3	////	4
4	ЖΤ	5
5	////	4
6	ЖΤ	5

4. How close was your prediction to the actual numbers?

Very close

5. Why do you think your prediction differed from the actual numbers?

Chance played a part in which number was on top.

MAKING MODELS

1. The nuts and bolts represent atoms and you will put them together to represent molecules. You will write formulas for each molecule. Use the following symbols:

Lo (long bolt)   Sh (short bolt)   Wg (wing nut)   Hx (hex nut)

2. Place a hex nut on a long bolt. The formula of this "molecule" is LoHx. If you add another hex nut, the formula is LoHx$_2$.

3. Use the nuts and bolts to make molecules and write the formula for each molecule in the chart below. Record how many nuts and bolts were used in each molecule model.

Molecule Formulas

Long bolts	Short bolts	Wing nuts	Hex nuts	Formula
/		/		Lo Wg
/		2		Lo Wg$_2$
/			/	Lo Hx
/			2	Lo Hx$_2$
/		/	/	Lo Wg Hx
/		/	2	Lo Wg Hx$_2$
/		2	/	Lo Wg$_2$ Hx
	/	2		Sh Wg$_2$
	/	/	/	Sh Wg Hx
	/	/	2	Sh Wg Hx$_2$
	/	2	/	Sh Wg$_2$ Hx
/			3	Lo Hx$_3$
/		3		Lo Wg$_3$

4. How are your formulas similar to those used by scientists for molecules?

They represent the kinds and numbers of nuts and bolts in combination. Chemical formulas represent the kinds and number of atoms of elements in molecules.

INTERPRETING DATA

1. Look at the graph of information about snakes of the world.
2. Answer the questions about the information in the graph. You may use the calculator.

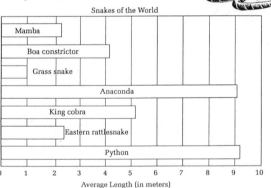

Snakes of the World

Average Length (in meters)

3. How long is the shortest snake?   _1 meter_
4. How long is the longest snake?   _9 meters_
5. What is the difference in length between the longest and shortest snake?   _8 meters_
6. How much longer is the anaconda than the king cobra?   _4 meters_
7. How much longer is the python than the boa constrictor?   _5 meters_
8. How much longer is the king cobra than the mamba?   _3 meters_
9. List the snakes in order from longest to shortest.

Python, Anaconda, King Cobra, Boa Constrictor, Eastern Rattlesnake, Mamba, Grass Snake

Student answers will vary. Please do each activity beforehand, as materials and equipment will affect outcomes. These answers are a guide to indicate trends you can expect in the data.

MAKING GRAPHS

1. Slide the rubber tube into the smallest water-filled beaker. When the tube fills with water, pinch one end closed.

2. Pull the pinched end out and down the side of the beaker until it is below the bottom of the beaker.

3. Release the pinched end over the large container.

4. Record the time required to empty the beaker.

5. Repeat the procedure for the other three beakers.

Siphoning Beakers

Beaker	Size of Beaker	Time Required to Empty Beaker
1	100 ml	25 seconds
2	200 ml	50 seconds
3	300 ml	75 seconds
4	400 ml	100 seconds

6. Graph the results of this activity. Title the graph, use numerals on each column to indicate the size of each beaker, and use numerals on each row to indicate the time required to empty each beaker. Label the columns and the rows.

Title _Time Required to Siphon Various-Sized Beakers_

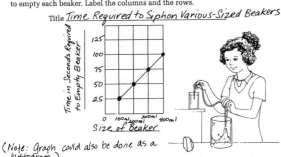

(Note: Graph could also be done as a histogram.)

HYPOTHESIZING

1. Estimate the order of the six objects from longest to shortest drop time when the objects are placed in the cylinder of water. Write the number of each object on the lines below.

Longest Drop Time ——————→ Shortest Drop Time
2   4   6   3   5   1

2. **Question:** How do the properties of an object (size, shape, volume, density, and weight) affect how fast it will fall through a liquid?

Your hypothesis (educated guess): _The objects that are smooth, small, and dense will fall the fastest through a liquid._

3. Drop each object into the cylinder of water and record how long it takes the object to reach the bottom.

Drop Times

Object Number	Drop Time
1	1 second
2	4 seconds
3	2.5 seconds
4	3.5 seconds
5	2 seconds
6	3 seconds

4. Order the six objects from longest to shortest drop time based on the actual drop times. Write the number of each object on the lines below.

Longest Drop Time ——————→ Shortest Drop Time
2   4   6   3   5   1

5. Which properties contributed to a fast drop time?

The properties which contributed to a fast drop time include small size, compact shape, and high density.

6. State the relationship between properties of an object and drop time.

The more compact and smooth an object is, the faster it will drop.

CONTROLLING VARIABLES

1. Add 1 teaspoon (5 ml) of salt to the 250-ml container of water. Stir until the salt is completely dissolved.

2. Record the length of time required for the salt to dissolve in the chart below.

3. Repeat this procedure using 2 teaspoons, 3 teaspoons, 4 teaspoons, and 5 teaspoons of salt. Important: Always start with fresh water before adding any salt.

Length of Time for Salt to Dissolve

Amount of Salt	Length of Time for Salt to Dissolve
1 teaspoon	30 seconds
2 teaspoons	50 seconds
3 teaspoons	65 seconds
4 teaspoons	80 seconds
5 teaspoons	95 seconds

4. Which variable did you change?
Amount of salt

5. Which variable responded to the change (what did you time)?
The length of time for the salt to dissolve

6. Which variables were kept constant?
Amount of water, manner of stirring, same timer, same container and stirrer

7. What did you find out about how the amount of salt affects the length of time it takes the salt to dissolve?
The larger the amount of salt, the longer the length of time for the salt to dissolve.

Student answers will vary. Please do each activity beforehand, as materials and equipment will affect outcomes. These answers are a guide to indicate trends you can expect in the data.

DEFINING OPERATIONALLY

1. Look at the diagram. Use the materials to construct a model of an insect.

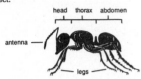

head thorax abdomen

antenna

legs

2. Describe your insect model to give your operational definition of an insect.

An insect is an animal with three body segments, six legs, and two antennas.

3. Look up *insect* in your science book or the dictionary and write the definition given in the book.

Any class of small invertebrate animals with three clearly defined body regions, head, thorax, and abdomen, with only three pairs of legs and usually with wings as beetles, bugs, bees, flies, etc.

4. How is your definition of an insect different from the definition given in the book?

My definition did not name the three body regions or give examples of insects.

Level 5   91

INVESTIGATING

1. **Problem:** Which of these magnets is the strongest? In this activity you will design and conduct an investigation to help you find out.

2. Describe what you will do to find out which magnet is the strongest.

I will place each magnet into a box of 100 paper clips and then lift the magnet and count the number of paper clips sticking to it. I will test each magnet 3 times and average the results for each magnet. I will graph the averages and use the graph to determine which magnet is the strongest by determining which picks up the most paper clips.

3. Construct a chart to show your results.

Type of Magnet	Number of Paper Clips Picked Up			
	Trial 1	Trial 2	Trial 3	Average
Horseshoe	81	62	79	74
Bar	47	54	64	55
Circular	42	38	43	41
Rod	3	4	5	4

92   Level 5

---

4. Graph the results listed in your chart.

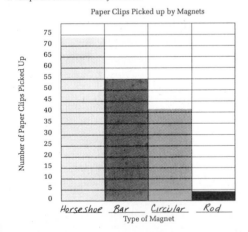

Paper Clips Picked up by Magnets

5. **Conclusion:** Which of these magnets is the strongest?

The horseshoe magnet.

6. What did you learn from this investigation?

I learned that the horseshoe magnet is stronger than the others. I learned that it is important to do more than one trial and average the results, since trials may vary. To tell which magnet is the strongest, they should be placed in the paper clips and lifted out in the same way. I learned that it is easy to tell which magnet is strongest by looking at the graph.

Level 5   93

OBSERVING

1. Use the senses of sight, smell, and touch to describe the mixture.

Color: White

Texture: Thick and gooey

Shape: Takes the shape of the pie tin

Odor: No distinguishable odor

2. Poke your finger into the mixture quickly. Describe what happens.

The mixture feels hard and my finger does not go through it.

3. Poke your finger into the mixture slowly. Describe what happens.

My finger goes through the mixture to the bottom of the pie tin.

4. Tap the mixture in the pie tin with you fist. Describe what happens.

The mixture feels hard and my fist does not penetrate it.

5. Pick up some of the mixture and roll it into a ball. Describe what happens.

The mixture rolls into a ball, but when I stop rolling it between my hands, it flattens out.

6. Pour the mixture into the container. Describe what happens.

The mixture pours slowly and takes the shape of the container.

98   Level 6

Student answers will vary. Please do each activity beforehand, as materials and equipment
will affect outcomes. These answers are a guide to indicate trends you can expect in the data.

COMMUNICATING

1. Describe the properties of the piece of popcorn (such as color, size, and shape).

   The popcorn is white with a darker center. It is irregularly shaped, soft, and about 2 cm in diameter.

2. Describe the properties of the kernel of corn.

   The kernel is yellow and shaped like a teardrop. It is hard and about 1 cm long.

3. Describe the differences between the piece of popcorn and the kernel of corn.

   They differ in color, size, shape, and texture.

4. Draw pictures in the boxes to show someone how to make popcorn.

5. Study your pictures. Did you forget any steps? Write them below.

   No.

ESTIMATING

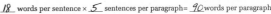

1. Open the science book to any page. Count the number of words in one sentence. Count the number of sentences in the paragraph. This is called a *sample* from the book.

   _18_ words per sentence × _5_ sentences per paragraph = _90_ words per paragraph

2. Multiply the number of words per paragraph by the number of paragraphs on the page. Use the area to the right to do your calculations.

   90 × 2

   Number of words per paragraph × number of paragraphs on the page = _180_

3. Open the science book to another page. Count the number of words in one paragraph. Count the number of paragraphs on the page. This is a sample of one paragraph.

   _74_ words in 1 paragraph × _4_ paragraphs per page = _296_ words per page

4. Multiply the result by the number of pages in the book.   296 × 403

   Number of words per page × number of pages in the book = _119,288_

5. Open the science book to another page. Count the number of words in two consecutive paragraphs. Count the number of paragraphs on the page. This is a sample of two paragraphs.

   _118_ words in 2 paragraphs ÷ 2 = _59_ words per paragraph ×
   _3_ paragraphs per page = _177_ words per page

6. Multiply the result by the number of pages in the book.   177 × 403

   Number of words per page × number of pages in the book = _71,331_

7. Devise your own method of sampling the paragraphs to estimate the number of words in the book. Describe your technique.

   Count all the words on a page and multiply by the number of pages: 170 × 403

8. Your estimate of the number of words: _68,510_ words

MEASURING

1. Carefully surround Lid 1 with a length of string. Then hold the string taut along the metric tape measure or meter stick and determine the circumference to the nearest millimeter. Record the measurement in the chart below. Repeat with the other lids.

2. Measure the diameter to the nearest millimeter of each lid by placing the metric tape measure or meter stick across each lid. Record the measurements in the chart below.

Lid Number	Circumference in mm	Diameter in mm	Circumference ÷ Diameter
1	350 mm	110 mm	3.18
2	260 mm	80 mm	3.25
3	710 mm	230 mm	3.09
4	330 mm	100 mm	3.30
5	290 mm	90 mm	3.22
6	230 mm	70 mm	3.29
7	110 mm	30 mm	3.67
8	210 mm	60 mm	3.50
9	260 mm	80 mm	3.25
10	90 mm	30 mm	3.00

3. For each lid, use the calculator to divide the circumference by the diameter. Record the result in the chart above.

4. Look at the results in the last column. What can be said about the result when the circumference of any circle is divided by its diameter?

   When the circumference of any circle is divided by its diameter, the result is about 3.14.

5. This is the value of the constant known as pi (π).

6. What is the relationship between the circumference and diameter of any circle?

   The circumference is about three times greater than the diameter.

COLLECTING DATA

1. Drop the tennis ball onto the table from a height of 100 centimeters and record in the chart below how high the ball bounces.

2. Drop the ball and record the distance it bounces from each of the following heights: 80 cm, 60 cm, 40 cm, and 20 cm.

Height from Which Ball Was Dropped	Height to Which Ball Bounces
100 cm	53 cm
80 cm	47 cm
60 cm	35 cm
40 cm	22 cm
20 cm	11 cm

3. Construct a graph of the data collected.

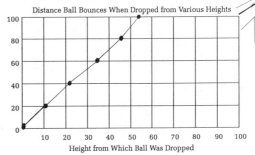

Distance Ball Bounces When Dropped from Various Heights

4. What is the relationship between the height from which the ball is dropped and the distance it bounces?

   As the height from which a ball is dropped increases, the distance the ball bounces increases.

Student answers will vary. Please do each activity beforehand, as materials and equipment will affect outcomes. These answers are a guide to indicate trends you can expect in the data.

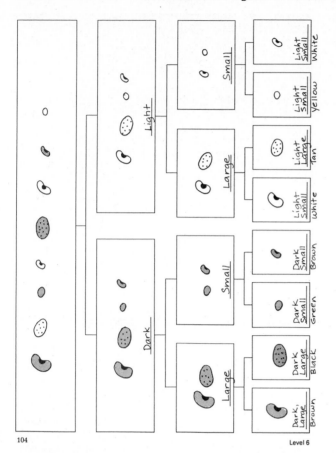

104

Level 6

INFERRING

1. Look at each cardboard shape and infer what three-dimensional shape would be generated by rotating it. Write the name for each three-dimensional shape or describe the shape in the chart below.

Two-Dimensional Shape	Three-Dimensional Shape Generated by Rotation
circle	Sphere
triangle	Cone
rectangle	Cylinder
ellipse	Ellipsoid (egg)
square	Double cone

2. Hold both ends of the strings in one hand and wind the shape with the other hand. Take one end of each of the strings in each hand and gently pull in opposite directions.

3. Observe the rotating shapes. How many of your inferences were correct? __5__

4. Write the name of the two-dimensional shapes that did not produce the three-dimensional shapes you inferred and describe or name the three-dimensional shapes actually generated by rotation.

They all produced the shapes I guessed.

105

PREDICTING

1. Use the eye dropper to place as many drops as possible on the penny until a drop spills over. Record the number of drops.

Drops of water a penny will hold: __25__ drops

2. Compare the size and shape of the penny with the other coins. Predict how many drops of water each of the other coins will hold.

Coin	Predicted Number of Drops	Actual Number of Drops
Nickel	30	34
Dime	20	18
Quarter	40	37

3. Test your predictions by using the eye dropper to place drops of water on each of the coins until a drop spills over.

4. If your predicted amounts did not match your actual amounts, what could account for the differences?

The height of the lip around the coin, the amount of the surface that is raised on the coin.

106

Level 6

MAKING MODELS

1. In this activity, you will make a model with your balloon to show how air particles move as air is heated and cooled.

2. Draw dots on the balloon with the marker.

3. Blow up the balloon and hold the end closed. Describe what happens to the dots as the balloon inflates.

As the balloon inflates, the dots get larger and move farther apart.

4. Slowly let the air out of the balloon. Describe what happens to the dots as the balloon deflates.

As the balloon deflates, the dots get smaller and closer together.

5. If this model shows how air particles move as air is heated and cooled, what do the dots represent?

Air particles

6. What does the process of blowing up the balloon represent?

The heating of air.

7. What does the process of letting the air out of the balloon represent?

The cooling of air.

8. Explain how this balloon model acts like the particles in air being heated and cooled.

As air is heated, the particles move faster and spread farther apart. As air is cooled, the air particles move slower and get closer together.

107

Student answers will vary. Please do each activity beforehand, as materials and equipment
will affect outcomes. These answers are a guide to indicate trends you can expect in the data.

INTERPRETING DATA

1. Look at the following table of information from *Consumer Reports*, September, 1987.

Paper Towels

Paper Towel	Price per roll	Towels per roll	Square Feet per roll	Cost per towel (price ÷ towels)	Cost per Sq. Ft. (price ÷ sq. ft. per roll)
Job Squad	92¢	50	40	1.84¢	2.3¢
Viva	83¢	90	71	.92¢	1.17¢
Bounty	96¢	88	73	1.09¢	1.32¢
Brawny	77¢	70	73	1.10¢	1.05¢
ScotTowels	74¢	124	88	.60¢	.84¢
Coronet	71¢	115	79	.62¢	.90¢
Hi-Dri	67¢	100	74	.67¢	.91¢
Zee	76¢	102	72	.75¢	1.06¢
Delta	59¢	110	75	.54¢	.79¢
Gala	76¢	110	77	.69¢	.99¢

2. Calculate the cost per towel of each of the brands. (Divide the price by the number of towels per roll.)

3. Calculate the cost per square foot of each brand of paper towels. (Divide the price by the number of square feet per roll.)

4. Which brand costs the least per towel? _Delta_

5. Which brand costs the most per towel? _Job Squad_

6. Which brand costs the least per square foot? _Delta_

7. Which brand costs the most per square foot? _Job Squad_

8. Which brand is the "best buy"? _Delta_
   Why ?_Delta is less per square foot, and less per towel._

Distance Dropped	Diameter of spot at widest distance (in mm)
10 cm	16
20 cm	20
30 cm	22
40 cm	24
50 cm	24
60 cm	26
70 cm	26
80 cm	28
90 cm	30
100 cm	32

Title _Water Drops_

(Graph: Diameter of Wet Spot in mm vs. Distance dropped in cm.)

8. State the relationship between the height from which you dropped the water and the diameter of the spot created. _The greater the height the water was dropped from, the larger the spot created._

HYPOTHESIZING

1. Hypotheses are educated guesses about the answer to a question. Give your hypothesis to answer the following question.

2. **Question:** What is the relationship between the height of the hole in the can and the stream of water coming from it when the can is filled with water?

   Your hypothesis: _The lower the hole, the farther the stream of water will come out of the hole._

3. Draw lines on the diagram to show how far the stream of water will travel from each hole.

4. Cover each hole with tape. Then test your hypothesis by filling the can with water and quickly removing the tape from each of the holes. Hold the can over the dishpan and observe the stream of water from each hole.

5. Draw lines on the diagram below to show the actual stream of water from each hole.

6. Was your hypothesis supported by your observations?
   Yes

CONTROLLING VARIABLES

1. Tape the pencil to the table so that half of the pencil is hanging over the edge.

2. Hang the rubber band on the pencil and attach the paper clip to the bottom of the rubber band.

3. Use the metric tape measure to measure the length of the rubber band. Record this measurement in the table below.

4. Place a washer on the paper clip and measure the length of the rubber band again. Record the measurement in the table below.

5. Repeat adding a washer, measuring the rubber band, and recording the measurement until all eight washers are on the paper clip.

The Stretching Rubber Band

Number of Washers	Length of Rubber Band
0 Washers	9 cm
1 Washer	13 cm
2 Washers	22 cm
3 Washers	31 cm
4 Washers	39 cm
5 Washers	45 cm
6 Washers	49 cm
7 Washers	52 cm
8 Washers	53 cm

6. Which variable did you change?
   The number of washers hanging on the rubber band (mass).

Answers   137

Student answers will vary. Please do each activity beforehand, as materials and equipment will affect outcomes. These answers are a guide to indicate trends you can expect in the data.

7. Which variable responded to the change (what did you measure)?

The length of the rubber band.

8. Which variables were kept constant?

Same anchor point, same measuring device, same manner of measuring.

9. What is the relationship between the length of the rubber band and the number of washers added?

The more mass (washers) added to a rubber band, the longer the length of the rubber band. The rubber band stretched most rapidly in the early stages of the investigations. The stretching diminished markedly at the end.

DEFINING OPERATIONALLY

1. Carefully open the peanut and separate the shell. Draw a cross section of the peanut in the box below.

Shell — Embryo
Skin — Kernel

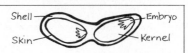

2. Carefully open the string bean and separate the pod. Draw a cross section of the string bean in the box below.

3. How are the cross sections of the peanut and the string bean alike?

Both are in a protective covering, both have kernels or seeds inside, and both are in pods.

4. The peanut and the string bean belong to a group of plants called *legumes*. Write your definition of a legume based on the characteristics that the peanut and the string bean have in common.

A legume bears its seeds in pods.

5. Look up *legume* in your science book or dictionary and write the definition given in the book.

The fruit or seed of pod-bearing plants, as peas, beans, etc., used for food.

6. How is your definition of a legume different from the book's definition?

I did not list examples of legumes.

INVESTIGATING

1. **Problem:** Which rubber band will stretch the most when 500 grams of weight are added? Design and conduct an investigation to help you find out.

2. Describe what you will do to find out which rubber band stretches the most when 500 grams of weight are added.

I will measure the width of each rubber band. I will attach a pencil to the table with tape and I will hang each rubber band from the pencil and attach 500 grams of weight. I will measure the length of each rubber band before and after adding the weight, find the difference, and graph the differences.

3. Construct a chart to show your results.

Rubber Band Width	Length before Weight	Length after Weight	Difference
2 mm	78 mm	380 mm	302 mm
3 mm	90 mm	230 mm	140 mm
5 mm	90 mm	130 mm	40 mm

4. Graph the results listed in your chart.

Title *Stretching Rubber Bands*

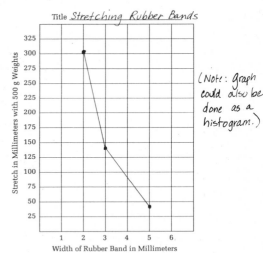

(Note: Graph could also be done as a histogram.)

5. **Conclusion:** Which rubber band stretches the most?

The rubber band with the smallest width.

6. What did you learn from this investigation?

I learned that the smaller the width of the rubber band, the more it stretches. It is important to attach each rubber band to the pencil and the weight in the same way. I learned that it is easy to tell which rubber band is strongest by looking at the graph.